SHIFT NATIONS THROUGH HOUSES —— OF —— PRAYER

by

Rick and Patricia Ridings

Founders, Succat Hallel 24/7 House of Prayer, Jerusalem

What others are saying about this book...

Shifting Nations Through Houses of Prayer, by Rick and Patricia Ridings, is a powerful book for every believer to read, especially those wanting to begin a ministry. In their founding Succat Hallel, God gave the revelation that it was not just about starting a house of prayer, but rather birthing it, in line with the timing and vision of God. Rick and Patricia's journey and lessons learned are a guide full of great wisdom for any type of pioneer work in the Kingdom.

Many of our Iris Global teams, including our last several Harvest Schools, have spent time praying at Succat Hallel. The presence of God is so strong there, we always want to stay for hours worshipping and praying while overlooking Jerusalem. I live in Mozambique, but I consider Israel another one of my home countries because my heart is so impacted each time I visit and pray there. I highly recommend reading this book and praying at Succat Hallel.

Heidi G. Baker, PhD
Co-founder and Chairman, Iris Global, Mozambique

I have known my friends Rick and Patricia Ridings for over twenty-five years. They are recognized elders in the global prayer movement who have the tested experience, biblical knowledge, and spiritual authority to write a book such as *Shifting Nations Through Houses of Prayer*.

This is not theory from novices. This book offers wisdom that can be gained only by a persevering lifestyle of long-term commitment to Jesus, and through costly experience. Anyone who can establish and sustain 24/7 prayer and worship in Jerusalem through the years of suicide bombings and other terrorist activities has clearly persevered in the faith and obedience required to give an authoritative voice to the truths in this book.

The authors provide practical insights and inspiring stories to help those who are called to pioneer a house of prayer in a challenging area with small numbers of local believers to serve with them. They also offer invaluable guidelines to those called to minister in other cultures.

Their book shares insights that are as precious jewels concerning Israel, the Middle East, and governmental intercession that will encourage more effective intercession from those who want to personally mature in their prayer lives.

I encourage you to read and meditate on this book, which I believe will minister deeply across cultures and generations.

Mike Bickle
Founder and Director, International House of Prayer, Kansas City
President, International House of Prayer University, Author

I am grateful for those who serve faithfully and sacrificially in essential roles of leadership. Rick and Patricia Ridings' commitment to the house of prayer movement undergirds all other endeavors.

They have been loving, patient and wise. They have overcome great difficulties and become a shining example to us all.

John Dawson
President Emeritus, Youth With A Mission

There is simply no book like this one, written by Rick and Patricia Ridings, on how to shake a nation through 24-hours-a-day prayer. It is both a training manual for around-the-clock intercession, and an invitation to become an intimate lover of God. I love this book, and you will too!

Dr. Cindy Jacobs
Founder, Generals International
Author, speaker

When Rick speaks, I listen. And so do many others. Rick and Patricia are a father and mother to the prayer movement in the Middle East, including houses of prayer in Turkey, where we received much from their ministry. Norine and I listen to Rick with confidence, because he embodies a rare combination of hearing God's voice along with a heart of wisdom and careful discernment. Together with this, he is a man of God marked by humility, obedience, and integrity. I do not exaggerate in saying that some of Rick's prophetic words have helped shape our ministry, and I have repeated them to many others. I recommend Rick and Patricia's book. I recommend Rick and Patricia! You will find that what they write is not theory. It is the fruit of full lives.

Pastor Andrew Brunson
Church planter in Turkey and imprisoned for his faith for two years

This book explains and gives understanding not only about the importance of houses of prayer for shifting in nations, but it also explains in detail the how-to of "birthing" houses of prayer in a nation.

Rick and Patricia Ridings stress the importance of "giving birth" to a house of prayer, rather than just starting or holding prayer house activities.

Reading this book is very exciting, because it includes life testimonies. I really appreciate their efforts in writing this quality book.

My prayer is that every reader will not only be blessed, but will also receive and carry the seeds of a house of prayer that in time will be "birthed"!

Dr. Niko Njotorahardjo
Senior Pastor, Bethel Church of God,
Gatot Subroto, Jakarta, Indonesia

It has been my great privilege to call Rick and Patricia Ridings my close friends for more than twenty-five years. Our paths first crossed in the early nineties in Brussels, where they had been faithfully paving the way for many strategic Kingdom initiatives on a European level during many years of prayer and worship.

When I helped found the European Coalition for Israel in 2003, Rick and Patricia were therefore some of the first people that I turned to for prayer and counsel. They immediately responded and agreed to take part in our first prayer conference, bringing together twelve intercessors from across Europe to pray the coalition into existence. This is only one example of their ability and humility to understand and be part of small beginnings, as they operate in the prophetic realm and are not limited by what the human eye can see.

Rick and Patricia have been fully committed to the Lord's call on their lives in changing the nations through prayer and worship. There are few books, if any, that I have been looking forward to reading as much as the one that you are currently holding in your hand.

Tomas Sandell
Founding Director, European Coalition for Israel
Brussels, Belgium

Our friends, Rick and Patricia Ridings of Succat Hallel, are a huge blessing to the house of prayer movement in Jerusalem and worldwide. We thank God for the wonderful unity we have in the prayer movement in Israel, and with the hundreds of congregations in Israel, and the thirty Isaiah 19 Highway nations.

We highly recommend *Shifting Nations Through Houses of Prayer*, for all who have a heart to see changes in their own lives, families, cities and nations.

Tom and Kate Hess
Jerusalem House of Prayer for All Nations, Mount of Olives Israel,
Founder, All Nations Convocation, Jerusalem, Authors and speakers

Jerusalem, the home of Rick and Patricia Ridings, is a world barometer, as we currently are entering a new time for the world prophetically. We must be on guard and awake.

We are entering the era when world-scale shakings are being revealed, and the greatest end-time wave of the Holy Spirit will soon be demonstrated to generations. The prayers of God's people are a powerful weapon that have heavenly authority to:

- » Unlock the nations.
- » Release the wealth of the nations to equip His saints to preach the Gospel of the Kingdom to the ends of the Earth.
- » Loose the biblical promises for this age.
- » Raise up new generations who will be filled up with the Holy Spirit and accelerate the fulfilment of the Great Mandate (Commission).

This book provides a deep understanding of the importance of our role in filling up the cup of God's grace with prayer and worship.

Daniel Pandji
Co-founder, Indonesia National Prayer Network
Co-founder, My Home Indonesia prayer initiative
Jakarta, Indonesia

CHI–Books
PO Box 6462
Upper Mt Gravatt, Brisbane
QLD 4122
Australia

www.chibooks.org
publisher@chibooks.org

Shifting Nations Through Houses of Prayer

Print ISBN: 978–0–6480116-9-9
eBook ISBN: 978–0–6485108-0-2

Printed in Australia, United Kingdom and the United States of America.

Distributed in the USA and internationally by Ingram Book Group and Amazon. Also available from other outlets like Bookdepository.co.uk and Koorong.com in Australia. Distribution of eBook version include: Amazon Kindle, Apple iBookstore, Koorong, Barnes & Noble NOOK and KOBO.

Editorial assistance: Anne Hamilton

Cover design: David Stone

Layout: Jonathan Gould

SHIFTING NATIONS THROUGH HOUSES

— OF —
PRAYER

by
Rick and Patricia Ridings
Founders, Succat Hallel 24/7 House of Prayer, Jerusalem

CHI BOOKS

With Gratitude

We are so aware that without the hundreds of worshippers and intercessors who have joined us as "watchmen on the walls of Jerusalem" in Succat Hallel over the past 20 years, we would never have become a 24/7 house of prayer. For each one of you, we are humbly grateful.

We would like to honor Martin and Norma Sarvis, who have stood with us since the beginning of Succat Hallel, and have been a source of strength and blessing through all these years.

We thank Susan Wittman for her many hours spent prayerfully editing this manuscript.

We also thank our wonderful daughters and their families who have worked with us, encouraged us, and sacrificed so much to see a house of prayer raised up that would overlook the Temple Mount in Jerusalem and be part of establishing His Throne in this "City of the Great King".

Dedication

This book is dedicated to the memory of our beloved daughter Esther Moore who "graduated" early, at the age of 29, after a long stand against cancer. She loved to worship and pray in the house of prayer, and is now part of the great cloud of witnesses who worship and pray around His Throne.

We were so blessed that she was able to read and give us valuable suggestions on much of this book. May her legacy continue through passionate worshippers and intercessors that will help shift nations and prepare the way for the King of Kings.

Contents

FOREWORD

I have given my life to preparing equipping materials to sustain the different movements of God in the earth today. While I might be most widely known for my contribution in the Global Prophetic Movement, my greatest love and passion in life is actually God Himself. Then it is my family. Next it is the place of prayer. I really have nothing worthwhile to say to anyone unless I have been with Him. So from my perspective, standing in the council of God is paramount for the success of any person, family, ministry, business or effective long-term endeavor.

There is absolutely no replacement for experience. Armchair coaches avail much in these days, but practitioners carry a different level of authority, wisdom and knowledge. Information abounds. But where are the sage voices that know these ways of God and can release an impartation that changes a person's life? What DNA is needed? What lifestyle is required?

In your hand you hold the writings of one of the wise men of this generation, Rick Ridings. Rick and Patricia live what they teach and teach what they live. This comprises a "voice that can be heard." Not only that, it comprises the qualities of a "voice that must be heard!"

I hear the voice of my Master saying, "Well done, good and faithful servants. You have kept your priorities right. I will now multiply the works of your years by raising up Generational Houses of Prayer through out the Middle East and beyond. You are a forerunner for the fulfilling of the Isaiah 19 prophecy being birthed in the earth today. I will now multiply your efforts through your leadership skills, training materials and media resources."

I have had the honor of being friends with Rick and Patricia for many years and have frequented their House of Prayer overlooking Jerusalem multiple times. Not only do I commend to you their life and international ministry, but also the penmanship of this book, *"Shifting Nations Through Houses of Prayer"*. This is a much needed equipping tool for today's Global Prayer Movement.

James W Goll
Founder of God Encounters Ministries
Author, Speaker, Communications Consultant and Recording Artist

INTRODUCTION

David's Legacy:
A Changed City and Nation

In mercy the throne will be established;
And One will sit on it in truth, in the tabernacle of David,
judging and seeking justice and hastening righteousness.
—Isaiah 16:5 (NKJV)

King David was just a man. He was a simple man, but he loved the Lord with all his heart, mind, soul, and strength. His story began as a worshipping shepherd boy, watching the sheep and praising his Creator. But that faithfulness and praise changed a nation and built a strong city.

When King David first started to reign in Jerusalem, he faced some enormous challenges:

- A nation that was still very divided
- A people who were still divided in their hearts between idolatry and worship of the God of Israel
- A nation surrounded by enemies who had been oppressing it and desired to destroy it
- A newly taken capital city that had strong foundations of idolatry

In the face of these great challenges, God gave David a simple but demanding solution: to establish what we would now call "a house of prayer." He was to bring back the ark of the covenant, which represented the manifest Presence of God. He was to erect a simple tent for it. He was to establish priests and Levites to worship and pray 24/7 right in the center of the capital, the hub of the nation's government, commerce, and arts.

By the end of King David's reign, through this "house of prayer," Jerusalem and the nation were united in serving the God of Israel and had rest from all of their enemies.

Three thousand years later, Succat Hallel is one of the houses of prayer watching on the walls of Jerusalem. We watch and pray overlooking the Temple Mount, worshipping the King Who reigns forever on that holy hill.

Just as David saw victories as he faithfully guarded what was entrusted to him, we have seen the Lord change hearts, cities, and nations through simple faithfulness, prayer, and praise.

And as He promised, the Lord is restoring *"the tent of David"* over all the earth (see Amos 9:11), raising up houses of prayer that worship and pray day and night, as they prepare the way and build up a throne for the great Son of David. In the meantime, His Presence is already changing cities and nations. We invite you to join the adventure.

PART 1

BIRTHING HOUSES —OF— PRAYER THAT MAKE A DIFFERENCE

CHAPTER 1

Houses of Prayer That Last

For whatever is born of God overcomes the world.
—1 John 5:4 (NKJV)

Spiritual Fathers and Mothers

When the Lord first spoke to us about birthing Succat Hallel in 1999, there were not many houses of prayer that we knew of. Yet in less than a decade, a few scattered houses of prayer became a global movement, indicating that the Holy Spirit is breathing upon the vision for houses of prayer. But if the Holy Spirit is breathing on this movement, why do we see many houses of prayer get off to what looks like a promising start, only to fizzle out within a year or two? We hope this book will help provide some answers to that question.

In our experience, houses of prayer that last and grow are first and foremost those that have been "birthed" and not just "started."

Preparation to Birth a House of Prayer in Israel

Rick and I first visited Israel in 1993 at the invitation of a European prayer leader who conducted international conferences there for many years. He knew we had been organizing citywide prayer gatherings called "Pray for the City" in cities all over Europe, Asia, and Africa. In preparation for these gatherings, we would first meet with the pastors and leaders in the city to ask them how they prayed for their city. As the leaders shared their prayer burdens and vision for their city, Rick would take notes, and write a proclamation unique to that particular

> In our experience, houses of prayer that last and grow are first and foremost those that have been "birthed" and not just "started."

city. In the gatherings we began "at the Throne" with praise and worship, flowed into prayers that the recognized leaders and pastors led, and ended with the prepared proclamation and blessing over the city.

Our friend from Europe invited us to one of the yearly conferences he helped lead in Israel with the idea that we would do something similar in Jerusalem. But we were in for a rude awakening. Jerusalem is not just another city! Soon after we arrived at the conference, one of the Israeli conference leaders said, "You can't do that here—we don't know you!"

That night I (Patricia) couldn't sleep. I remembered a prophetic word someone had given me when we were prayed over before coming to Israel: "The Lord will give you a song of deliverance to sing in Israel." As I tossed and turned, wondering why we had come to Israel, I thought, "Lord, I can't sing Israel a song of deliverance. I need *You* to sing *me* a song of deliverance!"

We had left our little three-year-old daughter, Esther, behind for the first time. She was in the hands of a very capable person, but still, I thought, "It's so hard to leave her for so long and so far away, and for what?"

Then I heard the Lord sing me the most beautiful lullaby: *"Hodu l'Adonai ki tov, ki l'olam hasdo. Hodu, hodu ..."* [*Give thanks to the Lord, for He is good, for His mercy endures forever.*] (Psalm 136:1).

I'd heard that song (composed by Israeli worship leader Batya Segal) for the first time that day during worship at the conference. It was as if the *Lord* sang it back to me so clearly in the middle of the night, and I fell sound asleep.

The next morning I ran up to Batya, gave her a big hug, and said, "Thank you for writing that beautiful song!" I told her what happened the night before. I felt so connected to her, because the Lord used the lovely song she had composed to comfort me and sing me to sleep. All the rejection I felt because of what the Israeli leader had said to me the day before just melted away, and I felt adopted and grafted into the natural olive tree, Israel. I think the Lord knew that I needed to feel what they feel (rejection from the nations) and to love them as the Lord loves them. They are indeed "the apple of His eye" (see Deuteronomy 10:8).

Further into the conference, while sitting in a meeting, suddenly I heard in my spirit the "song of deliverance" that had been prophesied I would give. I even heard the piano part very clearly. I asked the main leader of the conference if I could sing it, and he said yes. I asked the Israelis to stand, and as I sang this spontaneous, prophetic song, tears ran down the faces of the fifteen to twenty Israelis who were standing! The song was based on Isaiah 60: *"Arise, shine for your light has come, and the glory of the Lord has risen on you."* The song went on to say: *"Take off the rags of fear and rejection and put on the garment of praise."*

This moment joined us to Israel in a much deeper way than by doing a "Pray for the City" concert of prayer in Jerusalem. God's ways are certainly higher than our ways!

The pastor of Jerusalem House of Prayer for All Nations, Tom Hess, where 24/7 harp and bowl[1] worship and intercession has continued without ceasing since 1987, invited us to a gathering of Israeli and Egyptian leaders in Egypt that he was convening, and asked us to lead worship in English, Hebrew and Arabic. So right after the Jerusalem conference, we were whisked off to Egypt and onto the Isaiah 19 highway before we fully understood what was happening! (For more on the Isaiah 19 Highway, see chapter 16.)

What a privilege to participate in that historic Isaiah 19 gathering! The Lord gave us creative ways to weave together the few Hebrew

---

1   Please see English Glossary

songs we knew with some English songs, and working with a lovely Egyptian worship leader, we somehow led worship in three languages. What a whirlwind introduction to Israel and the Middle East! We realized we had so much to learn, and we were in awe how the Lord was directing our steps.

Rooted in the Land

After being joined to Israel in such a profound way, we felt more at home in Israel than any other place on earth. We knew that this was where we belonged, but it took several years of preparation before the Lord allowed us to actually move to Israel to birth a house of prayer.

We came to Israel almost every year after that first conference, sometimes with our three daughters. In May 1999, we came and stayed one month in a place called Shoresh, which in Hebrew means "root." Shoresh is a small community on top of a mountain in the middle of the country, with a panoramic view toward the Mediterranean Sea on one side, and a view of the hills of Jerusalem on the other. While looking over the valley, our daughter Anna, who was nineteen at the time, wrote the song "Four Winds" based on Ezekiel 37, which later was sung by the youth of Israel. The Lord was rooting us in the Land.

When our month-long lease was up for that holiday apartment, we accepted an offer to live in one of Roy and Mary Kendall's apartments on the northern border of Jerusalem. They were going away for the summer, and since they were a part of a city-wide prayer chain, they asked us to take their noon to two p.m. watch for them. Much of that summer Rick was ministering out of the country, so I gladly covered that time, sometimes by myself, and sometimes joined by our daughters, Anna and Esther. (Our oldest daughter, Bethany, was in university in the States.)

One day during this season, we were on Mount Zion in Jerusalem, looking down at Sultan's Pool. Bleachers were filled with Israeli girls wearing colorful T-shirts, and those with different colors were seated together. We asked a man walking by, "Who are these women?"

He said, "The beautiful women of Israel!" Then he told us they were soldiers graduating from the army. As we were standing there watching them, the Lord began downloading His will for the rest of our lives. He said, "I want to use your daughters in the coming youth revival in Israel, and if you live here, it will make it easier for them to live here. I want you to serve the youth in every way possible—praying for youth camps, making food for them, providing a place of worship for them, driving them around, praying for them, etc. And I want you to establish 24/7 worship and prayer in the spirit of the Tabernacle of David, within walking distance to the original city of David."

Wow! We were so amazed and thankful to hear His direction for the next season of our lives. We had come to Israel thinking we'd be going back and forth between Israel and the States, but the Lord said to put down roots, move to Israel and commit to building 24/7 worship and prayer. In response to what the Lord told us while looking down at Sultan's Pool on Mount Zion, we moved into a large apartment within walking distance of the original Tabernacle of David. We continued our family worship watch as soon as we moved in early January 2000, and on February 7, we opened the watches to the public.

Labor Pains

If, as we believe, the house of prayer movement has a purpose in these end times to prepare the way for the Lord's return, then we may expect there to be fierce demonic opposition to this strategic development. Just as Satan knew something was brewing, and sought to kill the baby Jewish boys in Egypt (see Exodus 1:16–22), and later in Bethlehem boys two years old and younger (see Matthew 2:16), we must be vigilantly aware that Satan will try to stamp out a house of prayer in its first two years of existence.

To overcome such demonic attack, a house of prayer must be "birthed" and not just "started." It's not enough to believe that the vision for houses of prayer is from God. It is not enough to desire to see such a house of prayer raised up in our city. Only that which is birthed in the womb of prayer—that which is *born of God overcomes the world"* (1 John 5:4 NKJV).

> A house of prayer is birthed when the Lord finds those who are willing to pay the cost of the long-term commitment implied in becoming a "father" or a "mother."

A house of prayer is birthed when the vision is given to us in a place of seeking the Lord for His will and timing in our lives. A house of prayer is birthed as that vision is confirmed by others. It is birthed as we carry that vision in our hearts until the exact moment the Lord says it is time to move on that vision, and in the specific ways He reveals to us to implement it. A house of prayer is birthed when the Lord finds those who are willing to pay the cost of the long-term commitment implied in becoming a "father" or a "mother." Many are willing to jump on the bandwagon of a trend to start a house of prayer, or to be a short-term "caretaker" for a vision, but that will not overcome the demonic opposition. Too many today want to add the vision for a house of prayer to the list of ministries in which they are involved. But that is also not enough to overcome the demonic opposition.

The Need for Focus

A main difference between a parent and a caretaker is focus. Parents know they must be prepared to make the sacrifices of getting up in the middle of the night to take care of their child; to do with less for themselves in order to provide financially for their child; to carry that child daily in their thoughts, their prayers, in their hearts.

When the Lord first spoke to us about starting Succat Hallel in 1999, He spoke about the need for focus—in other words, that we would need to lay down, for a season, almost all our itinerant ministry to the nations. After leading city-wide "Pray for the City" worship and prayer gatherings in many nations, sometimes with many thousands of people, suddenly we were being asked to lay all that down to meet with a small number of people in our living room.

Our friend Mike Bickle, founder of the International House of Prayer in Kansas City, said to me (Rick): "A lot of people talk about 24/7 houses of prayer, but you're one of the few I know who is actually doing 24/7. Did you ever think it would be so demanding? I've found the house of prayer requires more energy and focus than my church did when I was senior pastor of several thousand."

After the Lord raised up a strong leadership core in those first few years, we were able to take up some of our ministry in the nations once again. But even after almost nineteen years, we find that Succat Hallel, the "baby" that has now become a "child", demands a huge amount of emotional and physical energy from us most days. And we are more than happy to give it, because we are a father and a mother to this house of prayer, not just caretakers. We deeply admire and appreciate the many spiritual fathers and mothers we know who are paying the price to nurture houses of prayer in difficult places like Iraq, Egypt, Lebanon, and Turkey. Some even face persecution and the threat of martyrdom, but they refuse to abandon the "baby" that the Lord entrusted to them.

In some pioneering situations, the Lord may use "midwives." When the Lord called two of our leaders to Alexandria, Egypt, to help a house of prayer, there were already young adult Egyptians who were the spiritual parents of the work. However they needed "midwives" to help them fully birth the baby. They served there for three and a half years as "midwives," a long time for a birth. But when the Lord called them to another nation, the house of prayer had been born and survived, and had strong Egyptian spiritual parents to nurture and care for it.

> **There is room for many houses of prayer in larger cities–if they are walking together in unity.**

Walking in Unity for Our City and Nation

We are frequently asked whether there should be more than one house of prayer in a city. We believe there is room for many houses of prayer in larger cities—if they are walking together in unity.

There can be strength and blessing in the complementarities of different models and mandates of the various houses of prayer in a city. By the Lord's grace, we experience this in Jerusalem. We are so thankful that we can gather to worship, pray, and have fellowship meals with the leaders of the other houses of prayer in Jerusalem.

A Vision of Jerusalem's Houses of Prayer

In August 2000, soon after Succat Hallel began, I (Rick) was praying, and I saw a vision of the Old City of Jerusalem covered with thick darkness. It was like a deep, dark, murky fog covering the city. Then I saw four arms reaching up out of the ground from the north, south, east, and west around the Old City. Each arm had its elbow on the ground, with the forearm raised straight up, with the palm of each hand extended face-up. I understood that each arm represented a house of prayer, and was made up of worshippers and intercessors who were learning to flow together in ministry unto the Lord.

As these houses of prayer ministered to the Lord, I saw a throne descend out of heaven. Like ancient Middle-Eastern thrones, each foot of the throne was a golden, carved lion's paw. Each lion's paw of the throne sat upon the open palm of one of the four hands extended in worship and intercession. When the throne touched the hands, a golden, fiery substance like lava began to pour down over those extended arms. As it reached the elbows on the ground, everywhere it touched the ground became golden and glowing with the glory of God.

Then I saw this "golden lava" flowing from one arm to another, until it encircled the entire Old City of Jerusalem, representing the unity between the houses of prayer. When I shared this with Patricia, she remarked that from a heavenly perspective, it would look like a wedding ring around Jerusalem, expressing His eternal covenant with this city.

When this "golden lava" completely encircled the Old City, the Lord sat very strongly and deeply upon the seat of the throne, as if to say, "Finally, I have found a resting place for the weight of My glory." (The Hebrew word for "glory," kavod, implies the concept of that glory being weighty or heavy.) As the Lord sat down more deeply upon His throne, golden rain began to fall upon the Old City, and started to dissipate the dark clouds.

While there are more than four houses of prayer in Jerusalem, it's interesting that four main houses of prayer have been established in each of the cardinal directions. The Jerusalem House of Prayer for All Nations is on the Mount of Olives to the east. Succat Hallel is to the south. The Jerusalem (Pavilion) Prayer Tower and the Israel Prayer Tower are to the west. And Mishkant Tsiyon (a Korean 24/7 house of prayer) is to the north. The ones to the west and north were founded after I had the lion's paw vision.

I believe this vision is supported by the Word. In Psalm 22:3 (NASB), it is written: "Yet You are holy, O You who are enthroned upon the praises of Israel." And Psalm 132:8,13–14 says:

> 8 Arise, O Lord, and come to Your resting place, You and the ark of Your might. …13 For the Lord has chosen Zion, He has desired it for His dwelling: 14 "This is My resting place for ever and ever; here I will sit enthroned, for I have desired it."

It is very important that we honor the Lord's priorities and protocol and seek to walk in loving unity with other houses of prayer, and with the church and congregational leaders in our city. King David, the first "father" of a house of prayer, the Tabernacle of David in Jerusalem, knew this was key when he composed Psalm 133:1–3:

> 1 How good and pleasant it is when God's people live together in unity! 2 It is like precious oil poured on the head, running down on the beard, running down on Aaron's beard, down on the collar of his robe. 3 It is as if the dew of Hermon

were falling on Mount Zion. For there the Lord bestows His blessing, even life forevermore.

CHAPTER 2

Living Stones

You also, like living stones, are being built into a spiritual house to be a holy priesthood, offering spiritual sacrifices acceptable to God through Jesus Christ.

—1 Peter 2:5

The Right Team

Building a house of prayer requires praying in the right people. We stress "praying in," because this area of leadership is so foundational to the future that we cannot rely on our own wisdom or abilities to build a team. Only the Lord knows whom He has prepared to be part of the house of prayer, and He is the master builder. To build the temple, Solomon had his workmen chisel, shape, and prepare the stones of the temple in the quarry before bringing them to the temple building site. In the quarry they were shaped and formed to fit together perfectly with other stones, and only then were they brought together to be assembled (see 1 Kings 6:7).

We were amazed at the way the Lord sent so many leaders early on who could set certain foundations in place that would facilitate the long-term solidity and growth of Succat Hallel. This has enabled 24/7 worship and prayer to continue as of this writing for almost fifteen years.

A House of Prayer Starts With People, Not a Building

Succat Hallel is blessed today with a beautiful facility overlooking Mount Zion, the Temple Mount, and the Mount of Olives. But it was not always like that. For our first four years we had no central facility. During that time, we heard about a ministry that came to Jerusalem to start a house of prayer, and purchased a $1 million building! We remember asking the Lord why they had such an amazing place with seemingly only one person on staff, a caretaker, while we had no central facility, but "only" a team of several leaders meeting in our living room.

The Lord spoke to us that just as we are a "temple" built of "living stones," the house of prayer is not a place, but people—called and fitted together by the Lord Himself into a house of prayer. Many years later, we were deeply touched by a song written by our friend Eddie James that says, "Lord, make me a house, make me a house of prayer." He called us all individually to be a house of prayer, and then brought us together to build a corporate house with many rooms.

We asked the Lord to forgive us for the sin of comparison, and we began to thank Him for the wonderful leaders He had assembled around us in such a short time. We do not rejoice in what happened, but the $1 million facility never grew into a house of prayer. We believe it was because it was managed long-distance, had a "caretaker" rather than a spiritual father or mother, and the emphasis was laid on a facility rather than on "living stones."

Unity Comes by Waiting on the Lord Together

At the beginning of our house of prayer we had three public watches a week, from nine to eleven a.m. on Mondays, Tuesdays and Wednesdays. I (Patricia) led worship and Rick led in prayer. Soon after we began, the Lord brought quality leaders to us—four couples and a single lady of different ages, all of them worship and prayer leaders with the same burning heart for 24/7 worship in the spirit of the Tabernacle of David. We originally thought the Lord would send us many musicians so we could build a worship team. Instead, He sent us gifted worship and prayer leaders who were all called to lead watches. This laid the foundation for 24/7 much better than a single worship team with lots of instruments.

Although the leaders the Lord had sent to us were very strong, and no matter how much we all wanted to establish 24/7 worship and prayer, we felt led to start with just a few watches, and to do them *together*. We took turns leading, and resisted the temptation to try to cover as many hours as quickly as possible by dividing up. These times were so key in the building of the "foundation" of the house of prayer. Through the years we have weathered many storms, but the house stood strong because we took the time to worship and pray together from the beginning, even though we were coming from different streams, different styles of music and different church backgrounds. Nothing can knit such a variety of people together as tightly and surely as praying together, worshipping together, receiving prophecies together, supporting one another in all our differences, and waiting corporately upon the Lord.

We also decided early on that, instead of having a free flow of "whoever wants to lead", we should have a designated leader each day, and all of us would submit to his or her leadership for that particular watch. We had many powerful, profound and prophetic moments that first year in our living room.

Soon we began meeting in each other's homes, and added one more watch per week on Sundays from nine to eleven a.m. It was wonderful to go from house to house, to share and benefit from one another's gifts and hospitality, and to continue to build a deep bond of loyalty between us. This bond is the mortar that holds a house of prayer together, and these times were key in the building of the foundation of the house of prayer.

If you believe that your house of prayer is to become 24/7, you can sometimes feel pressure to try to add watches to the schedule too quickly. We decided early on that once we started a watch, we would continue that watch and always go forward, not backward. We slowly added watches over the years until suddenly we realized we were finally strong enough to sustain 24/7 prayer. Since that time, by the grace of God, we have never turned back!

In our own experience, there was a great amount of emotional investment needed for the birthing of each watch at the beginning. Because of the level of spiritual opposition in Jerusalem, we would

> A house built with living stones takes more patience and trust than building a physical house.

lead a two-hour watch and then need a two-hour nap afterward to recover the energy spent on that watch.

But a growing capacity for overcoming the spiritual opposition meant that, after a time, we could lead two watches for the same amount of energy as we did for one watch at the beginning. Later on, four watches could be sustained for the same effort. The Lord surely takes us *"from strength to strength"* (Psalm 84:7).

Recently, in a corporate watch, I (Patricia) received a spontaneous song: *"Build Your house, build Your house. Whatever it looks like, build Your house."* A house built with living stones takes more patience and trust than building a physical house. We are not building *our* house, we are building *His* house, and He knows exactly what He's doing! We had to continually say, "Not our will, but Yours be done." He sees the whole picture, so what may look to us as small beginnings, He sees as beautiful. We can honestly say that His work is perfect and all His ways are just, as we have seen Him add exactly the right "stones" in His perfect timing, and according to His master plan. Sometimes He even takes a stone or two away to use in another house for His greater purposes. This can be hard to deal with, but after a time, we have seen how He works all things together for our good.

Diverse Watch Leaders Attract Different People

As time went on, we realized that watch leaders with a vision for a particular kind of watch tend to attract others who are fairly similar in their anointing, burden, age, or language.

We found that certain worship leaders have a particular anointing that draws others who are hungry for that aspect of worship. They may well lead in other types of worship as well, but usually one area stands out. For example, of our early worship leaders, Patricia and I had an anointing for what I call "governmental worship"—worship that expresses the Kingship of Yeshua (Jesus), His Throne, and the establishment of His Kingdom or government over a city or nations. Nigel and Sandy Lidiard had an anointing for worship expressing the majesty and holiness of God. Martin and Norma Sarvis had a spiritual warfare mantle. Jon Mark and Sandra Davis had a "bridal" worship anointing. Anna Boyd had a "Father heart of God" and emotional-healing anointing. Hannah Korpela had an anointing for pure, worshipful intercessory dance. We often saw how dance was key to breaking through to higher praise, worship and warfare.

Among our foundational prayer leaders, there were specific burdens or emphases that drew together an intercessory core around them. For example, I (Rick) had an anointing in prophetic "seeing"—having many visions that provoke prayer, governmental intercession and proclamation. Hilda Chen had a burden for *aliyah* (immigration to Israel), and prayer for the nations. John and Una Gere had a burden and revelation for the Temple Mount, which led to a weekly on-site watch they led for many years, and which brought many to an understanding of that location's strategic importance in the end-time spiritual battles.

I (Rick) have noticed in some situations that many more women than men are drawn to the house of prayer. I highly value the priceless contributions to the houses of prayer that women bring. But if there are no men in the leadership, it will be difficult to draw men into the watches. Of course, the inverse is also true. And if there are only singles in the leadership, in my experience, it will be difficult to see married people drawn to the watches, and vice versa. If you are called to birth a house of prayer, it is important to pray for a diversity of leadership from the beginning, so that a balance of different types of people join the house of prayer.

In our particular context, as in many large cities today, another factor is language. Most large cities have a diversity of languages, so it is important that the house of prayer reflects that reality. But it is also very important to have watches in the language of the country in which we live. We thank the Lord for Martin and Norma Sarvis, Don and Anna Boyd, Efrat Gerlich, Adam and Bethany Rosenfeld, David

> God is a God of protocol. We are to show "honor to whom honor is due". The Lord will honor and give favor to our house of prayer when we show respect, honor and favor to others.

Seguin, Esther Moore, John and Tikva Ott, Zipporah Bennett, Joel Jelski, Stefan Mihaescu, Shiloh and Sarah Ben Hod, and others who pioneered Hebrew-language watches at Succat Hallel. Melad Khoury and Lamaan Naser pioneered in the area of Arab worship and prayer for the Arab world.

Over the years, we have had many wonderful worship and prayer leaders who have led watches in Amharic (the language of the Ethiopians), French, Korean, German, Russian, Chinese, and Spanish. We believe the heart of the Father is deeply touched as He receives worship in the different languages from the different peoples that He created.

It is important to have consistency, and as much as possible, for the same person to lead at the same time every week to allow each watch to build into a core of people. Our better-attended watches are definitely those that have regular leaders, and people usually know what to expect when coming to that watch.

Right Relationships With Local Spiritual Leaders

In the early foundational season of a house of prayer, it is vital to invest in right relationships with local congregations, other houses of prayer, key spiritual leaders, and leaders of other types of prayer ministries in the city. This is because we ultimately desire to build *His* Kingdom, and not our own "kingdom."

God is a God of protocol. The scriptures teach that we are to show *"honor to whom honor is due"* (Romans 13:7). When Abraham was called into the region where Melchizedek was already established as a king and a priest of the Most High God, Abraham honored him by bringing tithes, thus recognizing one who had been a forerunner before him (see Hebrews 7:1–2). *In like manner, we need to seek to know about—and to honor—those who have already been laboring to prepare the ground in our city or nation.*

I believe that the Lord will honor and give favor to our house of prayer when we show respect, honor and favor to others. How do we do this in a practical way?

Seek the Blessing of Local Leaders

It is good to make appointments with relevant local spiritual leaders to explain our call and vision to them, and to ask for their blessing. When we first felt the Lord was calling us to Israel, even though we were not sure at that point if it were long-term, I approached the two main leaders of the Messianic Jewish Alliance to ask them to pray and confirm whether they had peace about us moving to the Land. I even told them that we would not come unless confirmed by local leaders. To my great relief, when they got back to me, they said they felt we were called to Israel, and that it was long-term, not short-term.

When we first heard the Lord calling us to establish a house of prayer in Jerusalem to the south of Mount Zion and the Temple Mount, I contacted our friend Tom Hess who, some years before, had established the Jerusalem House of Prayer for All Nations on the Mount of Olives. We are so thankful that Tom gave us his blessing at the start of Succat Hallel.

Purposefully Network

We need to prioritize attending different types of "network" meetings to which we may be invited. Soon after our call to Jerusalem, I made an appointment with one of the key pastors whom I had already met, Wayne Hilsden. When I shared our call and vision with Wayne, he graciously offered to invite me to a fellowship of some of the pastors and leaders in the city. This opened the door to establish relationships with more pastors. When I was later invited to attend national meetings of pastors and leaders, it became an opportunity to build even more relationships. I explained to these pastors that our heart was not to "use" them to build our own ministry, but to seek to serve their congregations by training and bringing in more worship, prayer, and youth workers. They felt more secure when they were reassured that we were not there to "steal their sheep".

In Jerusalem, we who are leaders in houses of prayer try to get together every few months to fellowship, pray, eat, and worship together. These times are very important for keeping our relationships in good order.

Sometimes those in the houses of prayer isolate themselves from other types of prayer ministries. But there is great value in seeking to join networking gatherings of other prayer ministries. Others may approach certain things in different ways than we do, or they may not really understand what we are doing. But that is all the more a good reason for us to get to know one another and communicate our vision with each other.

I remember being invited to a Middle East networking meeting in our early days in Israel. I knew that some there probably would not have a heart for Israel, and I discovered soon after my arrival that that was very true, as they confronted me in a less than friendly way. I had to decide whether I would take the easy way out and just leave, or if I would talk, pray, and work through the issues with these individuals. It was not easy, but it was worth it, and over the years some of them have even become close friends.

Pray for Unity

It is important to pray for the unity of the local Body, and for local leaders. In Succat Hallel, we have always sought to make this a priority in our prayers. We have been quick to correct any new prayer leaders with us who prayed in ways that were critical of other houses of prayer, congregations or pastors. We have invited various pastors and leaders to share the vision of their ministries in our gatherings—and to receive ministry from them and to minister to them.

A while ago, a leader of a local ministry called to ask us to pray for him. He was asked to speak before a group that could prove to be rather hostile. He asked if he could come to Succat Hallel beforehand to share about it, so that our intercessors could pray for him. We were so blessed to be able to connect with the strategic work he was involved with, and to lift him up in prayer.

The blessing and security that comes from right relationships with each other in our individual houses of prayer, and also with groups and leaders of other ministries in the city is vital to building the foundation of a house of prayer that will last.

Apostolic and Prophetic Input

Another protocol of God is to value apostolic and prophetic input to the house of prayer, and even more so in the foundational stages. When the Lord says in 1 Corinthians 12:28 that He has set gifts in the Body, *"first apostles, and second prophets,"* I believe He is not setting these ministries on a pedestal. Rather, He is saying that their gifts are very needed, especially as a new community is being established.

Sometimes those called to birth a house of prayer operate in one or both of these gifts. But even then, there is value and wisdom in receiving input from others outside our house of prayer whom the Body of Messiah (Christ) recognizes as operating in these gifts, and who thus can more objectively perceive our situation.

I believe the Lord has gifted those with an apostolic anointing as builders who see and encourage people in their gifts, and how they relate to one another; who can give input as to relational difficulties; and who generally help to set things in order. I believe those with prophetic anointing are able to give words that encourage, build up, and exhort us in the direction of the Lord.

Nehemiah had an apostolic anointing to envision, gather, assign tasks, and build. But he and *"the elders of the Jews **continued to build and prosper under the preaching of Haggai the prophet and Zechariah** [the prophet]"* (Ezra 6:14; emphasis added). Here we see the need for (and the close relationship between) the apostolic and the prophetic.

In a house of prayer in the Middle East, we were asked several times to function in an apostolic or "fatherly" way to help them work through some early tests in the relationship between the main leaders. As we talked with the various leaders individually and as couples, we realized that a great amount of the strain in their relationship was because they were from different linguistic and cultural backgrounds. We explained some of the cultural differences and helped them overcome those hurdles. When one leader shared some things he had said to another leader, we explained that certain words he had used had a very negative connotation in English, and we asked if that was what he really meant to communicate. He was shocked when he found out the English word he had used had such a different meaning than what he had thought. As his English was good, but not advanced, we strongly encouraged him that when he spoke on "heart issues" with the other person, he should have someone there to translate from his language to English, and vice-versa. Later, after that relationship was healed, and the house of prayer was moving forward again, they greatly encouraged us when they said, "You were like a mother and father to us [to help us through the foundational times]."

May we not seek titles or authority, but simply and truly show "father" and "mother" hearts toward those with less experience than us. When we have not had much experience, may we have the humility to ask for the counsel and input of "fathers and mothers," and apostolic and prophetic ministries we trust.

CHAPTER 3

Preparing a Dwelling Place for the Lord

In that day will I raise up the tabernacle of David that is fallen, and close up the breaches thereof, and I will raise up his ruins, and I will build it as in the days of old.

—Amos 9:11(KJV)

When the Lord called King David to prepare a dwelling place for Him (the Tabernacle of David), God gave him very specific instructions about the timing and location. Three thousand years later, as we were standing on Mount Zion looking down into the Ben Hinnom Valley, the Lord told us He wanted to restore the fallen tent of David. We know that we are not the only ones called to this vision. But in obedience to this word of the Lord, we rented an apartment above the valley with a large living room where we could begin public worship and prayer watches to prepare a place for the Lord within walking distance of the original Tabernacle of David.

As we prayed about when to open our living room for public

> When the Lord called King David to prepare a dwelling place for Him, God gave him very specific instructions about the timing and location.

watches, we felt we should begin on 7 February 2000. Later, we learned from Jewish friends that this date was *Rosh Ḥodesh Adar*. In Hebrew, the first day of the month is *Rosh Ḥodesh* (*rosh* means "head," and *ḥodesh* means "month")—i.e., "head" or beginning of the month. We were not aware that this was a special time in the Hebrew calendar, and that often in the scriptures, significant events took place on the first day of the Hebrew months. We discovered long after we started our public watches that there are many examples of this in the scriptures (emphasis added in the following verses):

- Exodus 19:1 —**"On the first day** of the third month after the Israelites left Egypt—on that very day—they came to the Desert of Sinai."

- Exodus 40:2 —"Set up the tabernacle, the tent of meeting, **on the first day** of the first month."

- Leviticus 23:24 —"Say to the Israelites: '**On the first day** of the seventh month you are to have a day of Sabbath rest, a sacred assembly commemorated with trumpet blasts.'"

- Numbers 1:1 —"The Lord spoke to Moses in the tent of meeting in the Desert of Sinai **on the first day** of the second month."

- Numbers 1:18 —"They called the whole community together **on the first day** of the second month."

- Deuteronomy 1:3 —"In the fortieth year, **on the first day** of the eleventh month, Moses proclaimed to the Israelites all that the Lord had commanded him concerning them."

- 2 Chronicles 29:17 —"They began the consecration **on the first day** of the first month."

- Ezra 3:6 —"**On the first day** of the seventh month they began to offer burnt offerings to the Lord, though the foundation of the Lord's temple had not yet been laid."

- Ezra 7:9 —"He had begun his journey from Babylon **on the first day** of the first month, and he arrived in Jerusalem **on the**

first day *of the fifth month, for the gracious hand of his God was on him."*

- Nehemiah 8:2 —*"So* **on the first day** *of the seventh month Ezra the priest brought the Law before the assembly, which was made up of men and women and all who were able to understand."*

- The first day of each Hebrew month is also a time of revelation:

- Ezekiel 29:17 —*"In the twenty-seventh year, in the first month* **on the first day**, *the word of the Lord came to me ..."*

- Ezekiel 31:1 —*"In the eleventh year, in the third month* **on the first day**, *the word of the Lord came to me ..."*

- Ezekiel 32:1 —*"In the twelfth year, in the twelfth month* **on the first day**, *the word of the Lord came to me ..."*

- Haggai 1:1 —*"***On the first day** *of the sixth month, the word of the Lord came through the prophet Haggai to Zerubbabel, son of Shealtiel, governor of Judah ... 'Go up into the mountains and bring down timber and build My house so that I may take pleasure in it and be honored,' says the Lord."*

- In light of these scriptures, we were so amazed when we realized that the Lord led us to start on the first day of the twelfth month—the month of Adar. We asked the Lord why we "happened" to begin on the first day of Adar. As we searched the scriptures, we found that it was in the month of Adar that Esther, one of the greatest intercessors in the Bible, was used to bring about one of the greatest turnaround victories. Esther 9:1 (NASB) says that *"on the twelfth month (that is, the month Adar) ... the Jews themselves gained the mastery over those who hated them."*

As our 24/7 house of prayer sovereignly began on the first day of the month of Adar, we hoped, like Esther, to see victory over the Lord's enemies, and we prayed fervently for the salvation of Israel.

It was also significant to us that the Lord had us begin on the first day of the *twelfth month*, as the number twelve represents government.

Our main mandate in prayer is to pray for the government of God to be established on earth, specifically the House of David here in Israel, and for governments all over the earth to rightly relate to the House of David—the government the Lord is re-establishing here in Israel. So nothing ever happens by accident, and if we are sincerely seeking the Lord, He will allow us to move in His perfect timing!

An intercessor who came that first day brought an almond branch with blossoms—one of the first to blossom that year. In Jeremiah 1:11 (CJB), God asked, *"'Jeremiah, what do you see?' I answered, 'I see a branch from an almond tree* [Hebrew: *shaked*].*' Then Adonai said to me, 'You have seen well, because I am watching* [Hebrew: *shoked*] *to fulfill My word.'"* The Lord has been faithfully watching over us and fulfilling His word all these years.

The first day of our public watches we had a wonderful time worshipping together with about seventeen people in attendance. We expected the same group to continue coming. But to our surprise, not one person showed up the next morning. At first we were disappointed, as we thought we'd had a great time! But then the Lord said, "I thought these watches were about ministering to Me—I'm still here!" After repenting for our disappointment, Rick and I worshipped together and had a wonderful time with the Lord.

Afterwards, to console ourselves, we decided to go out for lunch. As we were walking to the restaurant, we saw a large room next to the Mount Zion Hotel. I found myself saying, "I think we should rent this place for watches."

Rick said, "Are you crazy? Not one person came to our watch today, and you want to rent this big room?"

But I envisioned Israeli youth worshipping there, and I said maybe we could rent it someday, and hire buses to bring Israeli youth there from all over Israel for extended periods of worship. That dream eventually came true!

The place we went for lunch that day had huge windows overlooking the Ben Hinnom Valley. The valley had been considered cursed by the Jews since the days of King Manassah, who encouraged the sacrifice of children to the false god, Molech. One area of the valley, *Topheth*, is from a word meaning "drum," and is thought to carry that name because people beat loudly on drums to drown out the screams of the children as they were sacrificed to Molech.

As the scriptures foretold, the valley had become a trash heap (see Jeremiah 31:40). As we looked down into the valley that day, we saw ladies dancing around a tree in a frenzied way, and we wondered if they were practicing witchcraft. We began to receive a mandate from the Lord to go down into the valley regularly to pray and to see that curse broken.

On the third day, the entire group who had come to our home to pray the first day came back. When we asked where they'd been, they said they'd all gone to hear a famous speaker who was in town. The Lord wanted us to know that the 24/7 house of prayer and worship He was asking us to establish was all about Him, not about people. And He also wanted us to understand that there was major cleansing needed in the Ben Hinnom Valley.

Spiritually Cleansing Our Geographical Area

After the Lord quickly drew our attention to the Ben Hinnom Valley, He showed us that we would never fully "break through up above" (on the hilltop) until we had broken through "down below" (in the valley itself). This revelation was rather daunting, as the Ben Hinnom Valley was not just an area where some witchcraft was practiced, but it was called in Greek *Gehenna*, another word for "hell". A curse had been pronounced over it in Jeremiah 7:31–33:

31 They have built the high places of Topheth in the Valley of Ben Hinnom to burn their sons and daughters in the fire— something I did not command, nor did it enter My mind. 32 So beware, the days are coming, declares the Lord, when people will no longer call it Topheth or the Valley of Ben Hinnom, but the Valley of Slaughter, for they will bury the dead in Topheth until there is no more room. 33 Then the carcasses of this people will become food for the birds and the wild animals, and there will be no one to frighten them away.

According to tradition, the valley later became a rubbish heap of continual burning, evidently what Jeremiah referred to when he called it the *"valley of the dead bodies and of the ashes"* (Jeremiah 31:40 KJV).

We realized something had to be done, not for fear of the witchcraft or demonic entities there, but in the fear of the Lord. We moved slowly on this, seeking to be led one step at a time.

In the next several months, we took many of our interceding friends down into the Ben Hinnom Valley to pray concerning the spirit of death. One day, we gathered there to pray together as a Jewish and Gentile group, repenting for the modern sacrifice of children called abortion (Israel has one of the highest abortion rates in the world). We felt God showed us that someday that valley would be filled with hundreds and even thousands of children and youth praising God. As we were leaving the valley, a little girl ran up to us and said simply: "Hi, my name is Tehelah!" Her name is the Hebrew word for "praise"!

We continued to take Israeli friends down to the valley to repent about abortion in Israel, and to worship the Lord God of Israel—the Lord of Life. We worshipped and repented of any way the spirit of death could be working in our own lives, and for the abortions that are so rampant in America and Israel. At a certain point, we started to walk further down into the valley, but we stopped, as some of us did not have a peace to continue. We went back up a little way to worship and praise, and we experienced a breakthrough of joyful dancing as we sensed the spirit of death was being broken.

As we were leaving the valley, we passed the place we'd been before, and there in the middle of the road was a dead, pale horse (a kind of light greenish-grey). That seemed pretty creepy to us. But after we arrived home, I felt to look in the book of Revelation, and found the passage about the pale horse that symbolized death (see Revelation 6:8). We suddenly realized and exclaimed to each other, "Something of Death has died in the Ben Hinnom Valley!"

Keys to Cleansing a Geographical Area

I (Rick) would like to point out some principles that are revealed in the prophetic history Patricia shared about the Ben Hinnom Valley:

First of all, we did not publically announce to any group or take just anyone who volunteered to go with us on this serious prayer assignment. We asked the Lord to guide us, and we believe He showed us each time which of the intercessors we were to take with us at that particular time of on-site prayer.

Second, we started primarily with repentance for our own sins as they related to the corporate sins that had occurred in that location. Then we acknowledged the corporate sins of our present-day people groups, acknowledging and pleading the mercy of the Lord over the historical corporate sin in that location. It was important for prayers concerning corporate sin that we had people praying (in this case, Israelis) who had the authority to stand in as representatives repenting on behalf of their own people, because they are descendants of those who committed the sins in that particular place.

Third, we sought to always move in total unity. Note that as shared above, how at one point we started to go further down into the valley. But we stopped and asked the Lord what to do when one of our team did not have a peace about continuing. As we prayed, the rest of us felt this same lack of peace, and that we were to continue to pray where we had stopped. We then saw a greater level of breakthrough.

Fourth, we praised and worshipped, and proclaimed the finished work of the Cross and the blood of *Yeshua Ha Masheah* (Jesus Christ) over that location.

Breakthroughs Down Below

As we began to see breakthroughs with the smaller teams, we started taking larger groups down to worship and pray in the valley. In September 2001, we went with a fairly large group to worship and to blow seven silver trumpets. The trumpets are scriptural weapons of warfare described in Numbers 10:9. *"When you go to war in your land against the adversary who attacks you, then you shall sound an*

Trumpets are scriptural weapons of warfare described in Numbers 10:9.

alarm with the trumpets, that you may be remembered before the Lord your God, and be saved from your enemies."

We did not know that the Second Intifada would begin that day, a period of attacks on Jerusalem by suicide bombers blowing up buses of innocent people, including children. It was clear that this particular battle was intensifying. Had we waited one more day to blow the seven silver trumpets in the valley, it might not have been possible because of the security situation.

But there were moments of calm, and the Lord continued to guide us to take teams to pray and worship, and to believe for the power of death emanating from the area to be weakened.

I (Rick) took a large group of young messianic believers further down into the valley. While they were praying for Jewish and Arab reconciliation, someone said, "Look up there!" And there on a ledge was a big, beautiful white stallion with no rider! He was brimming with life, and prancing around, looking down at the young people for about twenty minutes while they prayed.

Another principle of this kind of cleansing is to keep advancing with the power of worship, and proclaiming the lordship of Yeshua (Jesus) and relevant scriptures. That something was being accomplished in the spirit realm became obvious one day as we were worshipping, as Patricia shares below:

We continued to have weekly worship times in the valley as a community, meeting under the mulberry tree, praying, singing and dancing with the children. We had many amazing experiences in the Ben Hinnom Valley with Arab and Jewish youth. We often met Jewish and Arab children there, and they were drawn to the worship. We saw with our own eyes the meaning of the scripture, *"Through the praise of children and infants you have established a stronghold against your enemies to silence the foe and the avenger"* (Psalm 8:2). Once a man with an occult amulet and a rain stick tried to circle the children as they were worshipping. Rick asked him what he was doing, and he said, "There is only one kind of energy here—you need a balance of good and bad energy."

Rick told him we didn't need the bad energy! Just after that, the children began singing the chorus of *Alleluia*. When they sang "alleluia" and looked in the eyes of that man, he got really scared and ran away!

We were very encouraged to discover that the prophet Jeremiah, who had (at the Lord's command) pronounced a curse over the Ben Hinnom Valley, had also (at the Lord's command) prophesied a future time of blessing over that valley. In Jeremiah 31:40 (NASB), it is written: ***"And the whole valley of the dead bodies and of the ashes**, and all the fields as far as the brook Kidron, to the corner of the Horse Gate toward the east, **shall be holy to the Lord**; it will not be plucked up or overthrown anymore forever"* (emphasis added). We prayed not only that the curse over the valley would be broken, but we also proclaimed the blessing of the Lord, that it was to become a valley of "Life" rather than "Death." This was very important, as one of the major spiritual battles for Jerusalem is that of a culture of Life versus a culture of Death.

After three years of worship and prayer assignments in the valley, we saw an ad in the newspaper for a city tour of the Ben Hinnom Valley, so we decided to go and see what a secular Jewish tour guide had to say about it. Our guide didn't know us at all, but when we got to the valley he said, "As you know, the Jewish people considered this valley to be cursed because of the sacrifice of children to pagan gods, and *the way we knew it was still cursed is that birds did not come into this valley for hundreds of years. We don't know what happened, but about three months ago the birds came back, and that means the valley is no longer under a curse!"* Rick and I looked at each other, amazed at the vivid confirmation the Lord was giving us!

Since that time, not only have the birds continued to fly over this valley of Life, but even its physical appearance has greatly changed. The city of Jerusalem cleaned it out, and stopped dumping rubbish next to the mulberry tree where we had worshipped and prayed with the children. They made that area into a beautiful park, which today is one of the few places where both Jewish and Arab families can come to allow their children to run and laugh and play. They laid beautiful stonework around the park and down to the bottom of the valley.

One of the subjects of prayer in the prayer room above on the hilltop was for divine appointments with people. Part of the way the Lord answered this prayer was through our public worship in the Ben Hinnom Valley below. Because it was in the open air, people could come and hear the praise and worship. They would sometimes ask us questions and we were able to share with those who were hungry for the joy and life they felt in the worship.

Breakthroughs Up Above

As we began seeing breakthroughs "down below" in the Ben Hinnom Valley, we also began to see breakthroughs "up above", just as the Lord had said. A few months after we began in our living room, we were able to organize our first National Youth Gathering in the large room I had seen at the top of the valley on the second day of our public prayer watches. Our daughters, Bethany and Anna and their bands, along with other bands, led six hours of powerful, continual worship. Between 2000 and 2004, we had three or four of these National Youth Gatherings, most lasting six to eight hours. We bussed in youth from all over Israel, with around one hundred each time, and every time the Lord moved in powerful ways.

Suddenly, to our great disappointment, the hotel decided to turn the large room we were renting for these gatherings into a disco. During our four years of prayer and worship assignments in the Ben Hinnom Valley, we continued to take friends to lay hands on the doors of that room up above, even after it became a disco known as one of the darkest places in Jerusalem. Each time we prayed, we proclaimed over that contested room: *"The scepter of the wicked will not remain* **over the land allotted to the righteous"** (Psalm 125:3a; emphasis added). We took visiting intercessors there to lay hands on the building and to pray that we would be able to rent it 24/7 some day. It was ridiculously expensive, so at times we felt pretty crazy, but God is the

God of the impossible. Who would have thought He would indeed supply so abundantly that we would eventually be able to rent that same room for nine years of continual, nonstop worship and prayer!

As those four years of prayer and cleansing of the Ben Hinnom Valley drew to a close, one of the Succat Hallel intercessors, Mack McCoy—an architect who had a prayer assignment and vision for Mount Zion and the Ben Hinnom Valley—went with me (Rick) to look for a suitable facility for Succat Hallel. We had grown out of our facilities and desperately needed to rent something larger—even if it wasn't the room we had hoped and prayed for. We stopped by the Mount Zion Hotel and left my cell number with an employee who said he would ask if a room was available for us. Then we went on to look at other properties. We were just about to negotiate for another building we had been considering when the owner of the Mount Zion Hotel called and said, "The disco is going out of business. Would you be interested in renting that room?"

I had to conceal my excitement so I could get the best deal possible, and of course, I thought it was probably way too expensive anyway—but I found myself telling him we could give a down payment. Patricia continues to share:

When Rick came home with the news, we started praying, and what the Lord did next really surprised us. We thought perhaps we could find a businessman to help with such a huge amount of money. But one by one, intercessors started sacrificially giving. A few even suddenly received inheritance money and were able to give big amounts! The Lord wanted to use the Levites to provide the money we needed, and in so doing, for us to *own* the prayer room together!

Years later we can truly say that the Lord is fulfilling Jeremiah 31:40, and we are so privileged to be part of this fulfillment in our times. He will hasten His word to perform it—and cause even the Ben Hinnom Valley to be holy unto Him. Above the valley, a 24/7 house of prayer continues to worship, pray, and welcome the King of Glory to graciously come and dwell (tabernacle) among us.

CHAPTER 4

The Intergenerational Calling

One generation shall praise Your works to another,
and shall declare Your mighty acts.

Psalm 145:4 (NKJV)

A key principle of the Tabernacle of David that is often overlooked in houses of prayer is the calling to be intergenerational. I (Rick) believe the house of prayer movement will not come into its full potential without a revelation of the Lord's desire to see three generations walking, not in succession, one after the other—but in the godly synergy that comes when different generations learn to walk together.

A friend from mainland China shared with me a revelation he had received: that the concept of "succession"—passing the baton when we are at the end of our strength or life—is inherited from the pagan Greek worldview, much like runners in the Olympics pass the baton to the next runner. But the Lord showed my Chinese friend that the Hebraic worldview was for generations to learn to walk together, as seen in the lives of Abraham, Isaac, and Jacob. This linking of three generations is also encouraged in the New Testament

> **A key principle of the Tabernacle of David that is often overlooked in houses of prayer is the calling to be intergenerational.**

by the apostle John, when he writes in 1 John 2:12–14 to the "fathers," "young men," and "children."

In the Tabernacle of David, the intergenerational understanding was clearly lived out through the ministry of Levitical families:

> *1 David, together with the commanders of the army, set apart some of the sons of Asaph, Heman and Jeduthun for the ministry of prophesying, accompanied by harps, lyres and cymbals. Here is the list of the men who performed this service: 2 From the sons of Asaph: Zakkur, Joseph, Nethaniah and Asarelah. The sons of Asaph were under the supervision of Asaph, who prophesied under the king's supervision. .... 6 **All these men were under the supervision of their fathers** for the music of the temple of the Lord, with cymbals, lyres and harps, for the ministry at the house of God. .... 8 **Young and old alike, teacher as well as student, cast lots for their duties.** (1 Chronicles 25:1–2; 6, 8; emphasis added)*

In the Tabernacle of David, experience did not cause the fathers to monopolize the worship ministry; rather, they released and trained the younger worship leaders. Nor was the age of the fathers a cause for them to be put on the shelf; but rather, the younger leaders received instruction and oversight from those older and more experienced than themselves.

In these last days, as the houses of prayer are preparing the way for the Lord's return, it is significant that the Holy Spirit keeps speaking through so many about Malachi 4:5–6: "*See, I will send the prophet Elijah to you before that great and dreadful day of the LORD comes. 6 He will turn the hearts of the parents to their children, and the hearts of the children to their parents; or else I will come and strike the land with total destruction.*"

It is this turning of the hearts that will cause us to come into fullness as houses of prayer that are intergenerational communities. To walk in God's best, the older generation must make room for the next generation in a sacrificial spirit of humility. And the younger generation must honor and learn from the older generation with an equal spirit of humility.

Releasing the Younger Generation

After having the watches in our home for a few months, our daughter Anna received a vision to start a watch for youth on Saturday nights. At first there were just a few youth, but then it grew into a bigger group. In that group were some kids who grew up to be very influential Israeli leaders, including some who went on to write many Hebrew worship songs that are sung all over the country, and others who became professionals in the media and other fields. We believe those Saturday night watches made a difference in their lives. I remember how a group of them would walk from their congregation, which met downtown, all the way to Succat Hallel just for this weekly watch.

A few months later, Rick was supposed to speak at an international conference, but instead of speaking, he gave his time to praying for the youth. Judah Morrison from Haifa, and our daughter Anna from Jerusalem received prayer as they stood in to represent the youth of Israel. Many powerful intercessors from all over the world joined together to pray for youth revival. That very night, Anna was leading worship at a youth group "lock in" (an all-night party for the youth of a local congregation), when the Holy Spirit broke in! The kids worshiped for four hours, and their worship was the main event of the night. They were supposed to play games all night, and only sing a few songs, but they were hungry for God, and God showed up!

> **The battle will be strong for this present generation of children and youth, especially those with a Levitical calling to minister to the Lord.**

The Spiritual Battle for This Generation

If the intergenerational calling is really part of the end-time preparing the way of the Lord, as expressed in Malachi chapter 4, then we can naturally expect that we will not enter into it without a birthing and a battle. We can also expect that the battle will be strong for this present generation of children and youth, especially those with a Levitical calling to minister to the Lord.

One of the important mandates for the older generation in the house of prayer is to give ourselves, like Paul, to travailing prayer that will birth this generation into the fullness of their calling: *"My dear children, for whom I am again in the pains of childbirth until Christ is formed in you ..."* (Galatians 4:19).

We must not only "birth," but also *battle* for this most strategic generation. Satan is not unaware of the calling on this generation. He has released a mighty army of demons against them: spirits of abortion, drug abuse, sexual abuse, and even spirits of the fear of marriage and of having children.

We must receive strategies from the Lord to protect this generation, just as Jochebed, the mother of Moses, was led by the Spirit to hide him in a reed basket in the Nile River—and like Joseph, who was warned in a dream to take the baby Jesus down to Egypt until Herod died.

Wherever Satan has succeeded in snatching a child or youth into slavery to evil, we must not idly sit by. We must arise like David who, even when he was exhausted, refused to allow the enemy to keep the wives and children kidnapped by the Amalekites. You may remember this incident from 1 Samuel 30:3–4: *"When David and his men reached Ziklag, they found it destroyed by fire and their wives and sons and daughters taken captive. 4 So David and his men wept aloud until they had no strength left to weep."*

Drawing Strength From the Lord

David did not let the exhaustion he and his men felt after battle hold him back from chasing after his enemies to take back these stolen family members. In verse 10, about a third of his warriors were too tired to go in pursuit; but verse 6b says, *"But David found strength in the Lord his God."*

In 1 Samuel 30:17–19, when he miraculously discovered the camp of the enemy,

> *17 David fought them from dusk until the evening of the next day, and none of them got away, except four hundred young men who rode off on camels and fled. 18 David recovered everything the Amalekites had taken, including his two wives.* **19 Nothing was missing: young or old, boy or girl, plunder or anything else they had taken. David brought everything back** (emphasis added).

The Lord gave us a strong scripture that we have proclaimed many times as we battled to take back young people temporarily captured by the enemy. Isaiah 49:24–25 declares:

> *24 Can plunder be taken from warriors, or captives from the fierce? 25 But this is what the* LORD *says: 'Yes, captives will be taken from warriors, and plunder retrieved from the fierce; I will contend with those who contend with you, and your children I will save.'*

Releasing Children and Youth to Minister

We need to learn in the house of prayer to genuinely release youth and children to minister to the Lord. We found in Succat Hallel that when youth or children lead at least part of the worship or prayer, they join in much more fully. Three years after we started Succat Hallel, our youngest daughter Esther asked if she could lead a youth watch. So as we had said yes to our daughter Anna years earlier, we also allowed Esther, who was fourteen years old, to lead a watch with David Seguin, a budding worship leader who was even younger than her.

Although there is a certain risk in allowing youth to lead youth, we have found it is well worth the effort. Because they were leading, we prayed so much more for them, attended their watches, and interceded for them as they worshipped, wanting them to succeed and birthing them into their worship ministry at a young age.

In the meantime, our oldest daughter Bethany had finished university in the United States and came to Israel to produce a weekly TV show for youth, sponsored by Richard Frieden. This led to starting a youth ministry center called the "Jamm," where worship events and concerts were held specifically for youth. In Succat Hallel we prayed often for Richard Frieden's ministry.

Out of all this youth ministry grew the "Music Camps," co-sponsored by Succat Hallel and led by Bethany and Adam, our oldest daughter and her husband, to train youth to lead worship in singing and on their instruments.

The first camp lasted four to five days and, on the last night, the youth who attended were all encouraged to form worship teams. The music classes were divided into beginner, intermediate and advanced sections of piano, guitar, drums, and bass. The first four days they learned worship songs based on their ability. In the evenings a guest worship band played, and on the last night all of these youth teams took turns leading worship.

We remember the first evening of the camp, when only a small group of the youth were really entering into the worship. Many were acting up and not at all interested in worship. By the second meeting more entered in; and by the last meeting, when they all took turns leading worship, a powerful spirit of repentance fell. The meeting lasted late into the night, as the youth confessed and wept over their sins and re-committed their lives to the Lord.

We were invited to teach at a youth conference in Haifa, and we asked the youth to raise their hands if they wanted prayer to receive new songs. Sixty youth raised their hands! By God's grace, Bethany soon was able to put together a songbook of about eighty original Hebrew songs composed by Israeli youth, which are still sung today in congregations all over Israel.

After seeing our children released, years later we were praying for our grandchildren to become worshippers and to be wholehearted for the Lord. One of our young adult interns, Daniel, received a burden for our oldest grandson, Yoshi, who was eight years old at the time. He not only invited him to play football, but he also invited him to Succat Hallel to join in the worship. From one generation to the next, spiritual life, vision, and inspiration were being imparted.

During the worship, Daniel said to Yoshi, "Why don't we go up to the front and see if the Lord speaks to us?" Yoshi agreed, and after a while Daniel asked Yoshi if he received anything from the Lord. Yoshi said he saw "something like a vision." He said he saw himself and his friends in a dry desert place, and angels came and poured buckets of water on their heads! After that experience, he started taking guitar lessons, and a few years later that vision came true when he asked his mom, Bethany, if he could start a watch for himself and his friends. She very gladly said yes, and got involved in teaching them, praying for them, and supporting them as they led watches geared for children from ages nine to twelve. When he told his friends at school about it, they thought it was so "cool" that three of them came home with him after school so they could go to this watch. He started by playing one song, then two—and eventually he and his worship team could lead for about two hours, including spontaneous singing. Soon after starting this watch, most of his classmates were coming, and many wanted to be on the worship team!

We find that children and youth grow quickly in worship and prayer once they are encouraged and released. So, although there is adult supervision, we try to release more and more of the actual leading of the watch to the children. As of this writing, we have watches for children ages six to eight; nine to twelve; another for teenagers; and of course, many young adult watches.

May our houses of prayer be marked by a zeal for the youth, a spirit of mutual submission, and a humility that makes room for the young to learn and grow in worship and prayer.

Children and youth grow quickly in worship and prayer once they are encouraged and released.

CHAPTER 5

Spiritual Protection

But let all who take refuge in You be glad; let them ever sing for joy.
Spread Your protection over them, that those who love
Your name may rejoice in You.

—Psalm 5:11

Just as with physical parents and children, those who would "birth" a house of prayer must also be committed to its long-term welfare and protection. In my natural family, I (Rick) learned through a very difficult trial the value and necessity of daily praying a "hedge of protection" around my wife and children.

In 1983, when our first-born daughter Bethany was only five years old, we were ministering in Belgium—a country with strong spiritual oppression. I was speaking about intercession for the nation at a Youth With A Mission conference in Brussels. That evening, Patricia had stayed behind at the place where we were lodging—about forty-five minutes away. A Belgian lady there was ironing sheets on an old-style ironing machine that had a long cylinder covered in cloth. You place the sheet on it, and then a cylindrical hot iron piece comes down on it. Bethany was fascinated at this, seeing it for the first time. She did not realize how extremely hot the iron was, and before Patricia could stop her, she put her hand on the sheet just as the hot iron clamped down on it.

She experienced a very severe burn, and Patricia rushed her to the hospital. This was taking place at the same time that I was ministering in Brussels at the conference, when the Holy Spirit had come in a powerful way, and people were on the floor weeping for the nation.

By the time Patricia was able to contact me, Bethany was being examined at the hospital. Doctors said the burns were so severe that her hand would need to be kept in an oxygen tent for several days, and that she would almost certainly need extensive surgery on the hand to be able to have movement in her fingers again. I rushed to the hospital, only to find that the doctors wanted to keep Bethany isolated to avoid infection, and they would not even allow Patricia and me into the room. We could only look through the window, and weep and cry out for the Lord's mercy on this little five-year-old, who was bravely looking at the stories in her picture Bible.

The Lord intervened and healed her in a miraculous way, and she was released the very next day! She never needed surgery, and later she even played guitar, using the fingers of what she now called her "miracle hand." As she grew older, she did not even want plastic surgery for the scars, as she said they often opened a door of opportunity for her to share about the Lord's miraculous healing of her hand.

A Hedge of Protection

Even though this experience had a good ending, I did not want anything like it to happen to my family again, and certainly not during times when I was seeing the Lord break into meetings to minister in a powerful way.

As I sought the Lord about it, I came upon a teaching about praying every day for a "hedge of protection" to be around your family. It's based on the story in Job, chapter 1. Verse 5 explains Job's spiritual priesthood on behalf of his family: *"When a period of feasting had run its course, Job would make arrangements for them to be purified. Early in the morning he would sacrifice a burnt offering for each of them, thinking, 'Perhaps my children have sinned and cursed God in their hearts.' This was Job's regular custom."*

Later, when the Lord commended Job, Satan the accuser replied:

10 "Have you not put a hedge around him and his household and everything he has? You have blessed the work of his hands, so that his flocks and herds are spread throughout the land. 11 But now stretch out Your hand and strike everything he has, and he will surely curse You to Your face." (Job 1:10–11)

The Lord allowed Satan to attack this family in order to prove that Job did not serve the Lord only because of His blessing and protection: *"The LORD said to Satan, 'Very well, then, everything he has is in your power, but on the man himself do not lay a finger'"* (Job 1:12).

We all know the rest of the story, how Job's seven sons and three daughters were all killed by the collapse of the house in which they were eating. I believe that this was a test that legally showed Satan that there were those who would worship and serve the Lord no matter what. But I also believe we sometimes miss a very important point of this chapter: the norm for a believing father is to function as a spiritual priest to daily pray a hedge of protection around his family, which will keep Satan from being successful with his attacks against that family.

Once I saw this principle, I started each morning by praying a "hedge of protection" around my physical family. I began to see many situations where it was clear that the enemy had planned great evil against my wife or children, but it was cut short or averted. Then I realized that I also needed to pray such a hedge of protection around my spiritual family, those involved in the ministry we lead. Patricia will confirm that one of the first things I have done every morning for many years is to pray this hedge of protection around my family and those ministering with us. It is so much better to pray preventatively, rather than wait to "put on our armor" in the midst of a raging battle.

To help others practise this important discipline, I have provided below a sample of my own "hedge of protection" prayer:

O Lord, today and every day, according to the measure of Your infinite mercy and grace:

May Your hedge of protection be around us, the blood of Yeshua (Jesus) be over us, the whole armor of God be upon us, and as our days, so shall our strength be.

Please cleanse us from any sin, unrighteousness iniquity, idolatry, deception, or denial.

I pray that no weapon formed against us shall prosper or succeed: no witchcraft, no curses, no judgments, no evil speaking, no demonic assignment, and no "snare of the fowler."

Please protect us today from confusion, harassment, and division.

Protect us from spiritual, mental, emotional, or physical fatigue, injury, or illness.

I pray that no evil or unwise counsel of the world, the flesh, or the devil will prevail against us.

Thank you for protecting us today spiritually, mentally, physically, emotionally, in our finances, and our relationships.

May Your Holy Spirit, holy Word, and holy angels be released to us to help us walk humbly with You in faith, hope, love, holiness, justice, wisdom, and the fear of the Lord. Amen.

Dealing With Witchcraft

If we really believe that part of the calling on the house of prayer is to help shift the spiritual atmosphere over our city and nation, then we should not be surprised if the enemy sends those who try to work witchcraft against us.

Here in Israel, there is a particular kind of witchcraft that is not so difficult to discern, as people have actually left human feces on the doorstep of the house of prayer as part of a curse against us. We have found at those times that it has been important to call together a contingent of our spiritual leaders to:

1. Declare a spiritual cleansing of the house of prayer.

2. Declare we are grafted into the promise of Numbers 23:23—*"There is no divination against Jacob, no evil omens*

against Israel. It will now be said of Jacob and of Israel, 'See what God has done!'"

3. Declare that the power of the blood of Yeshua (Jesus) has delivered us from the power of any curses (see Galatians 3:13).

4. Re-install a "border" of the blood of Yeshua (Jesus) around the property. Sometimes we have taken the Lord's Supper and poured out the wine and scattered pieces of the bread over the property, in a prophetic act picturing and enforcing this protection.

Sometimes someone shows up at a watch who is operating in witchcraft. When this happens, there often will be an unusual amount of confusion or distraction in the room, and it will be extremely difficult to "break through" into the flow and peace of the Lord's manifested Presence. It's not always clear if this is because of witchcraft, but if there's even a chance that it is, I have found it is important to start singing songs proclaiming the power of the blood of Yeshua (Jesus). I occasionally have seen a visitor who I sensed perhaps was operating in witchcraft literally get up quickly and leave the room when we started singing about the blood of Yeshua (Jesus). After that, we seemed to easily break through into a place of joy and peace.

May the Lord give all leaders of houses of prayer the wisdom to daily pray a "hedge of protection" around their families and houses of prayer. May He give all leaders of houses of prayer the discernment needed to stop and reverse any kind of witchcraft or curses by the power of the blood of Yeshua (Jesus).

CHAPTER 6

Taking Back the Night

I have posted watchmen on your walls, Jerusalem;
they will never be silent day or night.

—Isaiah 62:6a

Why does the Lord ask for night watches? *Just as some prayer assignments call for fasting, others call for the sacrifice involved in night watches.* It is clear in the scriptures that in the end-time spiritual battle over Jerusalem, the Lord is calling for day *and* night watching in prayer.

The Purpose of Night Watches

Protection. It's very telling that the Bible says *the thief comes at night* (see Exodus 22:2; Job 24:14; Matthew 24:43; 1 Thessalonians 5:2), and that Satan is *the* thief. It's not difficult to see that Satan takes advantage of the night to tempt people to commit sins that they would not dare commit in the light of day. But in these days, the Lord is raising up a generation who will aggressively take back the night from Satan—and He is doing this through the establishment of night watches.

It was during the fourth watch of the night (3 a.m. to 6 a.m.), that Satan tried to kill the disciples of Jesus by sending a sudden ferocious storm on the Sea of Galilee. But as the battle against the disciples raged, Jesus kept a night watch in prayer (see Mark 6:42). He came out of this night watch to manifest His power and glory by walking on the water and calming the deadly storm.

Righteousness. Job 38 indicates that there is a time just before dawn to proclaim and set in place righteousness for the day, and a shaking out of evil:

> *"12 Have you commanded the morning since your days began, and caused the dawn to know its place, 13 that it might take hold of the ends of the earth, and the wicked be shaken out of it?"*

Meditation and Intimacy. The quiet of the night lends itself to meditation and intimacy with the Lord. David says in Psalm 119:147–148: *"I rise before dawn and cry for help; I have put my hope in Your word. My eyes stay open through the watches of the night, that I may **meditate** on Your promises"* (emphasis added).

> The Lord is raising up a generation who will aggressively take back the night from Satan–and He is doing this through the establishment of night watches.

In a marriage relationship, the night lends itself to intimacy and conception, as the night season is a time where there are fewer distractions. In the same way, one can experience a deeper intimacy with the Lord in the quiet of the night, and allow the "seed" of the Word to be planted in our hearts.

Hail Reserved for Times of War

We were led to add night watches in Succat Hallel even before we were able to fill all the daytime watches. Two years after we started our public watches, we felt that we should do the night watch together as a leadership team every Thursday night. On 28 March 2002, during one of these first night watches, I (Patricia) remember a very significant time. We decided to worship together for twenty-four hours, starting at six p.m. at Christ Church, where we had been doing a weekly watch on Thursday evenings. As we kept the watch, we had no idea that across the street in the Citadel of David, the prime minister and his cabinet were in an emergency meeting. They were deciding on a critical military operation ("Operation Defensive Shield") in response to a major suicide bombing that had just taken place at a Passover supper celebration in the city of Netanya. "Operation Defensive Shield" ended up proving very effective in dealing with the terrorist cells responsible for the Second Intifada.

As this strategic meeting was taking place, we were across the street singing a song I had written based on Psalm 68:4 and Isaiah 30:30–32:

> *Extol Him who rides on the clouds*
> *His Name is the Lord*
> *Arise, oh God, let Your enemies be scattered,*
> *Let the righteous be glad and rejoice*
>
> *The voice of the Lord shall be heard*
> *We will see His arm coming down*
> *With raging anger and fire,*
> *With thunderstorm, and hail*
> *To the music of tambourines*
> *He strikes with the blows of His arm*
> *His voice will shatter Assyria*
> *His scepter will strike them down*

As we were singing this song, it suddenly started hailing outside!

Around midnight, we moved to our Gihon prayer room to continue the watch. Early the next morning, without knowing what had happened the night before, the leader of the watch received Job 38:22–23—"*Have you entered the storehouses of the snow or seen the storehouses of the hail, which I reserve for times of trouble, for days of war and battle?*" As she was saying this, it began to storm again! Just after dawn that morning, I looked up at the sky, and in the dark storm clouds I felt the presence of the Lord. I felt enveloped by the clouds, and surrounded by the One who rides on the clouds. I remember thinking: 'We have nothing to fear; the Lord is so very near to us.'

That afternoon in the watch, someone read similar verses about hail and war, not knowing what had happened earlier that morning. Suddenly, it began hailing outside again! I remember scooping up the hail and holding it in my hand in wonder and awe at the confirmation the Lord had given us. When we finished that twenty-four hour period, we knew that the Lord had heard from heaven and answered our prayers. Very soon after that, we heard the news about the strategic physical battle that had been taking place at the very time we were singing and declaring these spiritual warfare scriptures.

His Faithful Provision for the Night Watches

We continued the Thursday night watches as a leadership team, but we were getting pretty worn out, as we all had busy schedules during the day. Then one day during a leaders' meeting, one leader after another said they had woken up at three a.m. We all thought that was strange, as it was not a Thursday night.

One of the leadership couples (Steve and Tonya Hansen) at the meeting said that they had also awakened at three a.m., and felt the Lord said they should change their schedule and do the night watch every night! For a few years, they faithfully carried the night watch in the apartment the Lord provided for us.

When Steve and Tonya had to return to the United States for their children's medical care, they passed the leadership of the night watch to a former intern, Lindy Heidler. We as a leadership team prayed over her, commissioning her for this new role and calling. We then entered into a time of spontaneous worship, and I (Patricia) started singing: "Fire in the night and a cloud by day." We sang that phrase together, over and over, crying out for the Lord's blessing and guidance. After that special time, I went home and composed the verses of the song, which seemed to express what we had lived out so far as a community seeking to establish 24/7 worship in the spirit of the Tabernacle of David:

You are God, there is no other
We are desperate for Your presence
We are pilgrims on a journey
Lead us, Lord and we will follow You
Fire in the night and a cloud by day
Fire in the night and a cloud by day

Lead us by Your Holy Spirit
Lead us to Your holy mountain
Let Your fire consume our darkness
Let Your glory fill our vision

Take us deeper, take us higher
Lift us up so we can see
Free us from our earthly bondage
Make us humble, set our spirits free
You are full of radiant beauty
You resound with ancient wisdom
We were fashioned for Your glory
We were made to worship only You
Fire in the night and a cloud by day
Fire in the night and a cloud by day

This is what we were after—not just 24/7, but *His Presence* 24/7—as a fire in the night and a cloud by day. It is what we as a community were living for, longing for, and watching the Lord establish before our eyes!

The Need for Dedicated Night Watchmen

I (Rick) have not yet seen a house of prayer go 24/7 that did not have dedicated night watchmen who were willing to adjust their schedules to take the night watches. As Patricia explained above, we tried to do a night watch once a week for three months, and it was important for all of us as leaders to experience the night watches. But those of us who did it felt we were on almost continual jet lag, and we realized the need for people who would be called to the night watch and adjust their schedules accordingly.

If most of the Psalms are a record of what happened in the Tabernacle of David, then it is clear David appointed some as night watchmen. Psalm 134:1 says, "Praise the Lord, all you servants of the Lord who minister by night in the house of the *Lord*." The Hebrew in this verse can be translated "who serve *nightly*," or "who stand in the house of the Lord *night after night*," or "who *by night* stand in the house of the Lord" (emphasis added).

These night watchmen were exempt from other duties, so they could keep the night watch: *"Those who were musicians, heads of Levite families, stayed in the rooms of the temple and were exempt from other duties because they were responsible for the work day and night"* (1 Chronicles 9:33).

The Value of Three-hour Shifts

After a period of time in which our night watchmen were doing six-hour shifts, they began to look a little pale, and the lack of exposure to sunlight seemed to be taking its toll emotionally. We felt we should experiment with two three-hour shifts: from midnight until three a.m., and from three a.m. until six a.m. Some people found that this worked much better, as they could get enough sleep either before or after their watches. They also could have the afternoon to get out in the sun and develop relationships with others who were not on the night watch.

While we encourage this three-hour shift model for the longer-term physical and spiritual health of the night watchmen, exceptions can be made. We realized some people prefer to stay for six hours instead of walking home in the middle of the night. So we now have a combination of night watchmen or women who do full nights (six-hour watches from midnight to six a.m.), and others who do three-hour watches (midnight to three a.m., or three a.m. to six a.m.)

Wailing Women

The night watches in Succat Hallel were pioneered by young adults, but when we went to shorter shifts, the Lord sent a wonderful intercessor, Nancy Claudio, more advanced in years, and very anointed in travailing intercession. She began leading the night watch and more "wailing women" joined her in filling the night hours. Wailing has to do with bringing forth or birthing what is on the

> **Wailing has to do with bringing forth or birthing what is on the Lord's heart.**

Lord's heart. Sometimes this is best accomplished in the privacy of a night watch.

Jeremiah 9:17–19a says: *"This is what the Lord Almighty says: 'Consider now! Call for the wailing women to come, send for the most skillful of them. 18 Let them come quickly and wail over us till our eyes overflow with tears and water streams from our eyelids. 19 The sound of wailing is heard from Zion...'"*

The Lord is raising up throughout the earth these dedicated night watchmen and watchwomen who are taking back the night from the enemy, and helping shift their city and nation into greater holiness and revival.

Our Times Are in His Hands

After fifteen years of living out 24/7 worship and prayer—as of the time of this writing—we are still dependent on the Lord, and must trust Him to send all the watchmen needed. One thing I (Patricia) have learned in administering the watch schedule is that the Lord cares about His house even more than we do! From the moment we said "yes" to Him, committing ourselves to keep the fire of 24/7 prayer and worship continually burning on the altar, He has always provided in miraculous ways.

We have seen this clearly manifested in the night watches. Many times, I said to Rick over the years, "I don't know if we can continue to have night watches—I don't see anyone able to do them." But the Lord is so faithful. Time after time, I received emails from intercessors who suddenly felt prompted to come to Jerusalem to do night watches just when we needed it the most.

The best example of obedience to these promptings is a lady named Leah Storset from Norway. On many occasions, the Lord spoke to her just when we were coming into a time when no one was available to do night watches. She would hear the Lord speak to her to "go to Jerusalem *now*," and she would drop everything and *go*! The old saying "Where God guides, He provides" is true.

We waited four years before we felt released to start 24/7 day and night prayer, and we never wanted to turn back once we started. The Lord strongly impressed on us that He wanted us to keep the fire burning day and night until He comes back again. We know that *"faithful is He who calls us, who also will do it"* (1 Thessalonians 5:24 NASB). We give Him all the glory for the miraculous ways He has provided and the wonderful people He continually sends to stand by day and night in His house. If you are leading a house of prayer, may He provide for you in the same miraculous ways.

CHAPTER 7

Joy in His House of Prayer

In Your presence is fullness of joy.
—Psalm 16:11b (NKJV)

It is significant that the main Bible passage from which we get the name "house of prayer" links joy in His house of prayer with Gentiles (non-Jews) coming to an understanding of the gift of Sabbath rest. The prophet Isaiah says:

*6 And **foreigners** who bind themselves to the Lord to **minister to Him**, to love the name of the Lord, and to be His servants, all **who keep the Sabbath** without desecrating it and who hold fast to My covenant— 7 these I will bring to My holy mountain and **give them joy in My house of prayer**. Their burnt offerings and sacrifices will be accepted on My altar; for My house will be called a house of prayer for all nations.* (Isaiah 56:6–7; emphasis added)

As Gentiles called to live in Israel, we found the Sabbath rest is not only a distinction that helps differentiate the Jews from other nations (like the covenant sign of circumcision). It's also a universal spiritual principle for all believers in all generations. *It is a gift that brings and maintains joy in the house of prayer.*

This principle is very simple: we all need to take one day a week off from our normal duties to experience that which will enable us to enter into the remainder of the week with fresh strength, peace, and joy. The Sabbath is not so much something to "do" as it is a gift to "receive."

> **The Sabbath is not so much something to "do" as it is a gift to "receive."**

The Sabbath predated the giving of the Law through Moses. One of our Israeli leaders, Norma Sarvis, (who has been with Succat Hallel since the beginning) says that Sabbath is a Creation principle, in that God could have stopped after the sixth day of Creation, but He made the seventh a day of rest, even for Himself.

The Israelites could not experience it during their slavery, when they toiled seven days a week. The first time the scriptures use the word "holy" concerns hallowing the Sabbath—keeping a day that is separate from the other six days of our week. On the Sabbath, we need to recognize and enjoy whatever is out of the ordinary for us, that which restores and recreates emotional strength, enabling us to resume our daily duties with freshness.

We are in this as marathon runners, not sprinters. Therefore, getting enough physical rest, times of recreation, and being able to laugh and enjoy life are not distractions, but are essential to our wellbeing. These things help us run a lifetime race of persistent seeking after God—to keep "burning" rather than "burning out." For these reasons, we seek to ensure that each of our staff has a weekly day off from the prayer room. We teach our core staff about the principle of Sabbath (*shabat* in Hebrew), and we emphasize that what is restful for one person may be different for another. We also encourage one day a week (for us, it's sundown Friday to sundown Saturday) in which most of our watches are more "soaking" or devotional in nature. We are not legalistic about this, but we try not to have intensive, strong intercession or prayer warfare on this day. To take one day a week of true rest enables us to keep running with joy. And, as Isaiah 56:7 says, our gracious Lord strongly desires joy to be a hallmark of His house of prayer.

God's Appointed Times

In Succat Hallel, we have discovered a great richness in celebrating the biblical feasts as well as the Sabbath. They reveal and renew our love for Jesus (Yeshua) the Messiah, who makes Himself known more deeply through His *"appointed times"* (see Numbers 23). They are a way to align ourselves with Him as we set our "spiritual clocks" here on earth to synchronize with the heavenly times and seasons of the Lord.

Celebrating the Biblical Feasts

As with the Sabbath, the Lord also gave the biblical feasts to help establish Jewish identity and to unify His people, foreseeing their exile throughout the nations. Yet they are much more than Jewish feasts— they are a revelation on earth of God's *mo'adim*, Hebrew for "appointed times." In Leviticus 23:2–4, the Lord says, 2 *"Speak to the Israelites and say to them: 'These are my appointed feasts, the appointed feasts of the Lord, which you are to proclaim as sacred assemblies 4 ... at their appointed times.'"*

The emphasis is on the fact that these times are "appointed" by God for us. That is why the enemy is so anxious to stop men from recognizing these appointments with God. As Daniel 7:25 says, *"He [the antichrist] will speak against the Most High and oppress His saints and try to change the set times and the laws."* In biblical Hebrew, "set times" is *zmanim*, also translated "appointed times"; and the word for "laws" (which is singular in the original Hebrew) also means "decree." It's interesting that even after Jesus returns to reign upon the earth, and He has fulfilled all things, there will still be celebrations of these appointed times of the Lord (such as the Feast of Tabernacles, or *Sukkot*, as prophesied in Zechariah 14.)

Recognizing the biblical feasts can bring freshness and focus into our worship and prayer watches. For example, the fifty days between Firstfruits and Pentecost (*Shavu'ot*) are known as the days of the Counting of the Omer (a unit of measurement, or grain offering). Firstfruits was fulfilled when Jesus rose from the dead, and Pentecost (*Shavu'ot*) was fulfilled when the Holy Spirit was poured out. That first outpouring of the Holy Spirit caused the fullness of the harvest to come forth. To celebrate the Counting of the Omer, one of our watch leaders, Martin Sarvis, sometimes placed one sheaf of wheat each day in a vase so we could watch the number of sheaves increase as we pray

> Another foundational principle of "joy in His house of prayer" is that it's not just about us –it's also about bringing joy to the Lord.

for a new Pentecost (*Shavu'ot*)—a fresh outpouring of the Holy Spirit to bring forth a great harvest in the Land. Our joy and faith increases as we see this visible countdown to the great harvest.

If we are to follow a calendar in the house of prayer, I suggest that the best calendar to follow is the one the Lord Himself established to let us know which dates are His "appointed times." In this way we can mirror on earth what is being celebrated in heaven.

Freshness in Worship and Prayer

Another foundational principle of *"joy in His house of prayer"* is that it's not just about us—it's also about bringing joy to the Lord. After all, it is *His* house of prayer. Ultimately, we are there for Him, to bring joy and pleasure to His heart. *We need to approach worship and prayer as we do marriage—purposefully arranging our lives to keep love fresh and evergreen.*

We keep our love for the Lord fresh as we grow in the knowledge of Him. He is like a vast continent on which we have landed, and which we have only just begun to explore. Nigel Lidiard, a friend who worked with us in the foundational years of Succat Hallel, was meditating on how the cherubim around the throne could continually exclaim: *"Holy, Holy, Holy is the Lord God, the Almighty, Who is, and Who was, and Who is to come"* (Revelation 4:8 NASB). He said he suddenly realized that they had a fresh revelation about God with each breath between their worship exclamations, and that each new revelation brought forth a new exclamation.

Knowing God

True theology is the study of God. There is great value in reading books such as *The Knowledge of the Holy*, by A. W. Tozer. Tozer takes one attribute of God at a time, and gives a short, but deep meditation based on some of the scriptures that speak of that attribute. I (Rick) know of no other book than the Bible that has so fed my spirit for over forty years. Inspired by Tozer, at certain seasons of my life I used a concordance to look up and meditate on scriptures about specific attributes of God—such as holiness, mercy, justice, faithfulness, sovereignty, goodness, etc. I then meditated on the scriptures, and wrote "love letters" to the Lord, each based on one of His attributes or titles.

As a community, we need to keep moving on with the Lord, and to inspire one another to keep seeking after Him. As leaders, we are to set the example, and receive fresh prophetic guidance and exhortation to help our community keep moving forward spiritually.

When we first moved to Europe in 1983, I noticed signs in the grocery stores proclaiming that the new wine for that year had arrived. It reminded me of Matthew 9:17, where Jesus spoke of new wine and new wineskins: *"Neither do people pour new wine into old wineskins. If they do, the skins will burst; the wine will run out and the wineskins will be ruined. No, they pour new wine into new wineskins, and both are preserved."*

As a community, we need to seek the Lord every year for both the new wine (spiritual freshness and revelation from the Holy Spirit), and the new wineskins (changes in structures of meetings to facilitate the new wine).

How many groups have camped around some revelation of the Lord and missed the next truth He desired to reveal about Himself? We must beware of the attitude that we have somehow "arrived", and that there's little more for us to know about the Lord. At one point I had felt rather smug, thinking I was ahead of certain other believers. He rebuked me and said: "You have only traded your little box for a medium box. I am much bigger than the biggest box you could

> Hunger for the Lord is not something we "work up," it is something we ask Him to stir up in us, and which we can then receive.

ever imagine. You must allow Me to continually stretch the limits of your understanding to grasp more of Myself as revealed in My Word." After a renewal experience with the Holy Spirit, I thanked Him for helping me realize He was so much greater than I had thought. I thanked Him for helping me take Him out of my little box that put such limits on Him in my life.

We as leaders must help our community to keep seeking after God, while avoiding spiritual pride or condemnation of others. We must follow after the Cloud of His Presence.

The true test of passion for God is not a one-time experience—it is to keep seeking Him diligently over the years and decades. We are truly passionate for Jesus when we overcome disappointments in life or in ourselves, and continue to press on to know Him. It is good to regularly pray for a renewed hunger for the Lord, and to purposefully position ourselves where we can receive. Hunger for the Lord is not something we "work up," it is something we ask Him to stir up in us, and which we can then receive.

Enriched by Other Gifts and Ministries

One wonderful aspect of the house of prayer is that we are not the only ones leading worship or prayer. It's good to attend watches led by others, where we can be inspired and stirred up to seek the Lord by what others have to give. In these watches, we are not distracted by responsibility for the watch, and we can press into the presence of the Lord.

Sometimes we also need to get out of our own environment and visit other houses of prayer, or places where the Lord is pouring out His Spirit. Some have criticized people who travel long distances to be touched by the Lord in a place where He is moving powerfully at a specific time. They say, "You should be able to receive the same thing here at home. After all, the Lord is here as well." I would challenge that way of thinking. I believe the Lord manifests Himself in specific ways, in specific places, and for specific periods of time. And I have seen that those who are hungry go to great lengths to *"taste and see that the Lord is good"* (Psalm 34:8 NASB). I believe He honors that kind of hunger.

At the same time, I would caution that we not try to copy or manufacture what the Lord is doing in a specific outpouring. We are not seeking a particular manifestation, but Him. Many years ago, I was helping lead a prayer conference in Italy, when some brothers arrived who had just been deeply touched by the Lord through the outpouring of the Holy Spirit in Argentina. After their testimony, we asked them to pray over us to impart this fresh touch from God.

As they prayed, the Holy Spirit came very powerfully. Some in the room started weeping, some started trembling, some experienced holy joy. I was disappointed when nothing seemed to happen to me. Then I realized I needed to stop seeking the gift, and instead start seeking the Giver. I closed my eyes, placed my arms out in a receiving position, and started worshiping the Lord, singing in tongues. As I was doing this, I felt someone pull on the hair at the base of my neck, forcing me to look upward. Then I felt strong hands lifting up my arms. I glanced to see who it was, but it was not a physical person. I sensed it was angels' hands holding up my arms. I closed my eyes and just kept worshipping. I felt such a deep restoration and strengthening. All this time, I physically felt those strong hands holding my arms up. After what seemed like a few minutes, I opened my eyes, and realized Patricia was the only one still left in the room. I had stood with my arms stretched out straight for over an hour. I left that place feeling refreshed and full of new grace.

The Freshness of Diverse Anointings

We keep life in our worship as we expose ourselves to different anointings. I have sometimes noticed that a specific worship leader or even an entire worship movement seems to have a strong anointing in a specific area of worship. The same is often true of different worship leaders in a house of prayer. One has a special anointing for worship that is majestic, bringing a strong sense of the holiness of God. Another is anointed for joyful, childlike praise, or for strong warfare, and apostolic or prophetic proclamations. Another is anointed for very quiet, intimate bridal devotion. Rather than comparing ourselves to others, it's good to be thankful for the variety of anointings in the Body, and seek to expose our spirits to the different aspects of God manifested under each of these anointings.

On a practical level, especially for worship leaders, it is good to expose ourselves to different styles of music. Many of us develop an emotional attachment to songs and styles of music that were popular when we were teenagers, or that were commonplace when we first came to the Lord. Most of us probably have specific songs that still touch our hearts deeply. However, they may not have the same depth of meaning for others. The Bible has a reason for saying often in the Psalms (the record of what took place in the Tabernacle of David): *"Sing unto the Lord a new song"* (Psalm 98:1 KJV; emphasis added).

This does not mean that we cannot use old songs. In fact, there is great value in using both old and new. This is made clear in the statement of Jesus that *"every teacher of the law who has been instructed about the kingdom of heaven is like the owner of a house who brings out of his storeroom new treasures as well as old"* (Matthew 13:52; emphasis added). For those called as worship leaders or musicians, sometimes just learning a song in a new or different style releases something new inside us.

Releasing Creativity

Expressions of creativity release new life and joy into the house of prayer. Our God is *the* Creator, and He is continually creating. Because we are created in His image, we are not satisfied in our spirits when everything becomes predictable.

In the Tabernacle of Moses, the Tabernacle of David, and the Temple (the three major expressions of God-ordained worship in the Old

Testament), artistic expression was greatly valued. When the Lord first prepared His people for corporate worship, He instructed Moses to assign much of the artistic work to the skilled artist and craftsman Bezalel, saying in Exodus 31:2–4:

> ## The Lord has anointed the art of dance and banners to release breakthrough in worship.

2 See, I have chosen Bezalel son of Uri, the son of Hur, of the tribe of Judah, 3 and I have filled him with the Spirit of God, with wisdom, with understanding, with knowledge and with all kinds of skills— to make artistic designs for work in gold, silver and bronze, 4 to cut and set stones, to work in wood, and to engage in all kinds of crafts (emphasis added).

Houses of prayer can take inspiration from Bezalel's example. Beautiful paintings hang in our worship room, bringing revelation and inspiring worship, since the Lord is not boring, but creative, why should the rooms where we worship and pray look boring?

In a similar way, the Lord has anointed the art of dance and banners to release breakthrough in worship. I love what a worship leader in England said when asked why he danced in worship. Rather than a lengthy theological discourse, he simply answered, "I dance in worship because I cannot fly!"

Those who are truly anointed for worship dance do not draw attention to their dance technique or their bodies, but rather, they lift our eyes up to the Great Artist who created the gift of dance.

I (Rick) grew up in a church tradition where you didn't "go to dances." I understand their desire to move away from the impurity often expressed in dance in the world. But it is sad that they missed the joy and pure beauty of true worship dance. When I first started studying the Tabernacle of David over thirty years ago, I was struck by the prominence given to dance in the Psalms. I thought: "That needs to be restored," but I also thanked the Lord that He would never ask me to dance, as that was way out of my comfort zone.

He spoke to my heart and said, "I would never force you to dance, but it is a way of worship revealed in My Word, and it would bless Me if you wanted to express worship in that way to Me." I was at home when I had this revelation. I locked the door to the room, pulled down the window blinds, and awkwardly tried to dance to the Lord, still feeling very uncomfortable. At a certain moment, the Holy Spirit came on me. I started whirling around the room singing and dancing, and I felt an amazing release of joy in worship. I felt like someone had just opened the door of my cage, and I could finally fly like I was created to!

Creativity also releases new joy into the house of prayer as we step out to sing or play spontaneous or prophetic new songs to the Lord. Both the Psalms and the book of Revelation, the two foundational worship "songbooks" of the Bible, encourage us to "sing a new song" unto the Lord. I have often experienced a release of life and joy as a worship leader, both when I learn a new song, and when I sing a spontaneous song to the Lord.

A Continual Walk of Faith

Another key that releases joy in the house of prayer is walking in faith. When the Lord asks us to step out in faith in circumstances that involve taking a risk, it's because He wants to fill us with joy as we experience His faithfulness in a new way.

For example, at one point in Succat Hallel we had become very comfortable in the room where we began night and day worship and prayer that had continued for nine years. Suddenly, the door unexpectedly opened for the possibility of a different room. To change rooms after so many years and with so many people involved would obviously mean a lot of disruption, and also new steps of faith for us. But as we prayed about it, we felt it was a "governmental shift" that was really important to the Lord. The result was that we moved to a room with a direct view of the Temple Mount. This continually reminded us that our praise and worship is very much to be part of "establishing" or "building up" the Throne of David on His holy hill. One day, Jesus will sit as the Son of David on that throne to bring the peace of His Kingdom to the nations of the earth (see Psalm 2:6–8; Isaiah 9:7). As a community, something fresh is released each time we step out in faith, seeking to follow the Cloud.

Generosity

Another core value that brings joy is generosity. Something very special happens as we learn to walk in generosity. What a joy to give, and what a joy to receive! How blessed we were recently when one of our older couples felt the Lord wanted them to give their car to a young family who really needed one. And what a joy for that young family to receive a car! This is a core value we need to model as leaders if we want to see it become a characteristic of our community.

> **Something very special happens as we learn to walk in generosity.**

Creating a Culture of Grace

If there is one element that distinguishes houses of prayer marked by joy, it is that they have sought to develop a "culture of grace." It is significant that the Greek word often translated "joy" or "delight" is *chara*, which literally means "joy because of grace"; (the Greek word *charis* means "grace").

As a student in Bible college, this link between grace and joy, and conversely, between legalism and unhappiness, was visibly demonstrated to me during ministry at a nursing home. There, I met an old woman in a wheelchair who had no teeth, and whose limbs were twisted from arthritis. One would have understood fully if she had been depressed and complaining. But instead, she shone with grace and joy as she explained to us that her "ministry [was] to bring joy to people." Rather than judging and complaining about the atmosphere and the service around her, she was continually encouraging and thanking others.

In stark contrast was a man who was visibly quite healthy for his age, and who should have been joyful about that. Instead, he judged others and complained about everyone and everything. His judgmental attitude created a cloud of gloom around him.

If we are quick to find fault with others, we will inevitably create a culture of legalism, resulting in an oppressive atmosphere of discouragement and heaviness in the house of prayer. But a culture of gazing on the grace of the Lord, and receiving and demonstrating that grace to others is certain to lead to *"joy in His house of prayer."*

In Exodus 34:6, in one of the clearest definitions of His character, the Lord reveals Himself to Moses as *"the compassionate and **gracious** God, slow to anger"* (emphasis added). If our Lord, who is Truth, says that graciousness is a foundational element of who He is, then let's pray that those who come into our houses of prayer will sense an authentic culture of grace—resulting in great joy.

CHAPTER 8

Keys to Building the House of Prayer

The priests and Levites—everyone whose heart God had moved—prepared to go up and build the house of the Lord.

—Ezra 1:5

The Role of Interns

About two years after we began the watches, a young couple named Steve and Tonya Hansen moved to Jerusalem to join us. They had a burden to lead an internship for young people who wanted to become "watchmen on the walls." We found a beautiful house to rent for the internship and we tore down walls on the bottom floor to make a prayer room. This became known as the "Gihon house."

One highlight of that spring internship was when they all went by ship to Russia to pick up Russian Jews who were making *aliyah* (immigration to Israel). They practiced many songs and dances, as they were asked to do performances on the ship to entertain the new *olim* (immigrants). These immigrants had left their families and friends behind to move to a faraway, unknown place called Israel. One intern composed and performed a beautiful song about *aliyah*, which in Hebrew literally means "going up to the Lord" or "going up to Jerusalem".

The ship was one way the Lord used to expose the interns to local believers. Israel is always bustling with life in different ways, so in every internship there is a different set of events, feasts and opportunities to experience the Land.

A few years ago, we decided to call our internships the "STAND Program". God is calling people from every tongue and tribe to come up to Jerusalem to "stand" before the Lord in worship and prayer; to "stand" as watchmen on the walls of Jerusalem (see Isaiah 62:6); and to "stand" "in the gates of Jerusalem". As King David says: *"I was glad when they said to me, 'Let us go into the house of the Lord.' Our feet have been standing within your gates, O Jerusalem! ...That is where the tribes go up ... to give thanks to the name of the Lord"* (Psalm 122:1–4 NKJV).

After we chose the name, I (Patricia) thought of an acronym for STAND: Standing Together, Announcing the Nation's Destiny. The STAND watches are late in the evening, so our interns are *standing* by night in the house of the Lord. For three months they live, eat, worship, and experience the land of Israel *together, announcing* what the Word of God says about the *nation's destiny*.

The enemy wants to steal, kill and destroy in the night hours, when so much sin and compromise takes place. But the interns claim those vital hours of the late evening for the Lord as they pray for His will to be done in Israel as it is in heaven.

The local Israelis have to get up early in the morning to go to work, so we thank the Lord for the "Standers" who can be fresh and awake for the late evenings because they are able to sleep a little later in the morning than the locals. We don't begin our corporate morning meetings until ten a.m., so the interns can join in these morning watches and still feel like they are part of the community. After they attend the ten a.m. morning watch, there's time to eat lunch, listen to a teaching from one of our staff or a visiting teacher, and then rest or take a nap so they'll be fresh for the late evening watch.

Watching during the late evening hours is a gift of love to God, but it is also a safe time when the interns can develop skill on their instruments and in leading worship without a lot of people coming into the prayer room. In addition to these late evening times, the interns join some of our staff worship leaders in the daytime watches to learn from them and to serve others by helping out with the song projection and sound systems.

Internships and Training

Although the STAND Program demands a time investment from the leadership in terms of teaching and oversight, it brings fresh troops to the battlefront who breathe renewed life and joy into the house of prayer. The internships have not only been key to recruiting more people to lead watches, they are also a valuable way to introduce the house of prayer as a possible short- or long-term calling for those who complete the program. After sixteen years of providing internships for a few hundred participants, a large percentage have returned for short-term visits to cover watches for us, often at moments when we really needed their help. Since our first internship, we've received new recruits every three months for the past sixteen years!

The internships have also been a way for us to sow into the Kingdom of God and into the global prayer and worship movement, as many have returned to start or strongly bless a house of prayer back home. For example, we had a few internships for leaders from mainland China. A few years after our first small Chinese internship, I (Rick) spoke at a Chinese conference. The leader asked people to come to the front who had started, or were part of a house of prayer in China, because they or their leader had interned at Succat Hallel. I was amazed at the large number who responded!

A clear time period for an internship (for us, it's three months) means that the leadership team and the intern will both have time to know whether or not he or she is called to join the house of prayer. By the end of this period of time, it is usually clear whether or not the intern should be accepted, should he or she apply for a staff position.

In our house of prayer, the Lord showed us that the internships were not to be a "discipleship training school" requiring a lot of pastoral care, but that we should only accept those who had already gone through some kind of personal restoration, emotional healing and character development. We require that everyone wanting to do the internship fill out a lengthy application, which usually reveals whether or not the applicant has received some sort of basic discipleship ministry.

The Value of a Good Application

Much time can be lost in draining situations arising from one intern or staff person who was not really sent by the Lord to your house of prayer. Over the years, we developed a thorough application to help us get to know potential interns or staff in advance. The application can be downloaded from our website. In addition to many pages of questions, we also ask them to send a written testimony, and to provide reference forms filled out by both their pastor and a personal friend.

Over the years, we have grown more cautious about accepting interns and staff. With time, we realized we are on a battlefront, and those needing a lot of healing are better off going to a ministry called to be a spiritual hospital than to come to a frontline spiritual battlefield. Perhaps a potential intern may someday have the calling to come to us, but sometimes we need to recommend they first go through foundational training elsewhere.

In this regard, it is better to build slowly but surely, with the right people. Most staff members we have accepted from outside the country have completed our internship program, or spent time with us as short-term volunteers. Most of our local staff have been involved in our watches as volunteers for a number of years. If there's some question, or we don't know the person well enough, we suggest they come on staff for a three-month trial period, after which either of us can say whether it's best for them to join us or not.

Casting the Net for More Worshippers and Intercessors

As we have visited and ministered in houses of prayer in different nations and continents, we have seen that many grew at first through the network of relationships of their founders. But at some point, they reached a plateau, and their staff numbers leveled off because they were not reaching beyond that original network of relationships.

So how can we "cast the net" to expose the ministry of our house of prayer to a larger number of people? The Lord accomplished this for us in an unexpected way.

Early on, a lady from Christ Church who came to our watches told her pastor, Michael Cohen, about Succat Hallel. She suggested that I (Patricia) lead worship for Christ Church on Sunday mornings. I met with him and he asked me to be the new worship leader. What a privilege it was to lead worship in the oldest Protestant church in the Middle East, which was founded to minister to the Jewish people!

Soon after I began leading Sunday worship, we started leading a Succat Hallel worship watch in Christ Church on Thursday nights. We met people from all over the world who were staying in the Old City. During one of the Thursday night meetings, Rick had a vision of water coming out of the stones of the floor. It was gushing underground from Christ Church to the Temple Mount, bringing living water to the Jews at the Western Wall, as well as to Muslims on the Temple Mount. He also had a vision of youth going from Christ Church to Ben Yehuda Street in central Jerusalem with tongues of fire on their heads, pushing back the spirit of death. We had many powerful watches in this strategic place. It was a wonderful experience to serve there, and through it, many people learned about Succat Hallel.

Expanding the Vision

In one Middle Eastern nation, we helped an indigenous house of prayer that was started by three local young adults who shared a hunger for more of God. They started watches in an apartment, drawing from their network of friends, and experienced great blessing. But after a time, they reached a plateau, as there were no more interested young adults in their network of relationships.

Around that time, I (Rick) felt led to strongly encourage them to start a more "public" meeting one night a week as a focal point to which they and their friends could invite others. They found a local international congregation that was willing to receive them and to support their effort. This one public meeting a week in their language became a clear doorway into their house of prayer. Word spread among local believers about this meeting. Here, the house of prayer leaders found potential new volunteers for their watches in the apartment. They could invite those potential volunteers without the problem of attracting difficult or indiscreet people to their house of prayer, which needed to stay under the radar because of security and persecution issues in their nation. They broke through their plateau or "ceiling," and once again began to grow.

Another way to cast the net is through special events. When a visiting guest speaker or worship ministry leads one or several special meetings, you can invite a broader spectrum of the believers in your city. Such events can become a focal point for those who may have heard about your house of prayer to finally come and visit.

These kinds of special events also can provide further training and fresh input to those who are already part of your house of prayer. At the same time, they are a natural way for them to invite friends who might become interested.

Relational Networks

Relational networks are numerous and common in some nations, and rare in others. If you live in a place with various relational networks, it's worth investing the time of some of your leaders to participate. Examples are: meetings for pastors and ministry leaders; intercessory prayer networks; men's or women's ministry networks; regional or national conferences or seminars; youth leaders' meetings, etc. All these are opportunities for divine appointments where, as you pray, the Lord will help you find others with a similar heart and vision for prayer and worship.

Local Staff and Financial Support

We relate to several houses of prayer in the Middle East, and we encourage them by providing regional training seminars, sending short-term staff or teams, and being available for counsel.

One challenge many of them face is how to see more indigenous believers become part of the house of prayer, especially if it was started by foreign workers. We also faced this in the past, but because of our emphasis on youth ministry to locals, we have made substantial progress in the past few years. In our case, each of our local volunteers has led one to two watches a week. These have been a great blessing and helped us have more watches in local languages—in our case, Hebrew, Arabic, Amharic (Ethiopian), and Russian. Over time, local pastors reported that these people were better able to lead in worship or prayer in their local congregations as a result of their experience with us.

However, we had in our hearts to have more than just a "token" number of local, indigenous staff. Patricia and I prayed earnestly about this for some time. At a certain moment, we felt the Lord say the basic problem was that the local congregations in our land are not yet large enough to support those called to minister in the houses of prayer (our international staff raise their own support). He showed us that we should step out in faith to raise a basic amount of support for each local young adult to come on staff.

Around that time, Michael Cohen, one of our watch leaders, went home to be with the Lord. We were touched by the sensitivity and love of his wife, Fran. To honor his memory, she started a memorial fund to provide financial support for young Israelis to be on staff. Her late husband loved young people and was very loved by them, so this was a very precious way to honor him. We see her as a pioneer in releasing young Israelis into their Levitical calling to minister to the Lord. Around that time, I (Rick) shared the vision of supporting local staff with a couple of Chinese believers from Hong Kong. They both committed to give a monthly amount for this purpose.

These two generous gifts helped jump-start us in this area. As we shared the vision in different nations, more people felt the Lord lead them to commit a monthly amount to support Israeli young adults in the house of prayer. We explained to potential Israeli staff how much we could provide as a foundational "salary," and that they would need to raise the rest of the support they needed, like our international staff.

Integrating more indigenous staff into our house of prayer has rooted us much more deeply into the nation of Israel, and we believe it has given us greater authority and understanding in praying for this nation and region.

CHAPTER 9

Repairing Strained Relationships

Bear with each other, and forgive … as the Lord forgave you.
—Colossians 3:13

Even if we seek with all our hearts to establish a culture of grace in the house of prayer, there will be times when we need to face up to and deal with strains in relationships.

Over the years, I (Rick) have found there are three distinct steps needed to see healing in relationships: *First*, go to God about the relational strain; *second*, deal with the spiritual warfare against the relationship; and *only then*, speak directly with the person involved. Let's examine these three areas more fully:

First, go to God about the relational strain. I believe we need to seek the Lord about the relational strain before approaching the person in question. When I skipped this step, I sometimes spoke strong words out of deep emotion, which ended up making the strain even worse.

As we go to the Lord, it's good to start with our own need, and ask Him such questions as, "Where is there a similar problem in my own life?"—and "What do You want to say to me in this situation, Lord?" Perhaps we don't have the exact same problem in our own life, but we may have the same root sin, such as pride or selfishness. We need to ask the Lord, "What did I do wrong, or what needful thing did I neglect to do in this situation?" Proverbs 18:17 explains that *"in a lawsuit the first to speak seems right, until someone comes forward and cross-examines."* The Lord, as the only perfect Judge, is able to reveal to us what we would not normally see about ourselves. He alone can help us even begin to see what happened from the other person's perspective, and not just from our own.

Before the Lord, we also need to choose to forgive the person for the way he or she wounded or offended us. This is a choice, not just a feeling. In fact, we can make this choice in obedience to the Lord, even before we feel forgiveness.

As a young person, I was deeply impacted by a story by Corrie ten Boom, whose family was betrayed by someone as they were helping to hide Jews from the Nazis in the Netherlands during World War II. Corrie, her father, and her sister were all sent to a concentration camp as a result. While there, her father and sister died from the horrible treatment. By a miraculous clerical error, Corrie was released shortly before she would have been gassed.

After the war, Corrie ten Boom went to churches and gave her testimony of how the Lord had enabled her to forgive even her enemies. Once, while speaking in a German church, a man came up to her and explained he had been an SS guard in one of the concentration camps. He had since come to the Lord, and had repented and received the Lord's forgiveness. He said it would mean a lot to him if Corrie would shake his hand as a sign that she also forgave him.

What he did not realize was that Corrie recognized him as one of the guards who had terribly mistreated her and her sister, who had died. She said her first emotion was an urge to "shake his neck" rather than to "shake his hand". But immediately the Lord reminded her that we have been forgiven the "unforgiveable" sin of causing the death of His only begotten Son because of our sins. She made a choice to forgive this former SS guard, despite still feeling great hatred. But she said that when his hand touched hers, a waterfall of healing washed out so much pain from her heart that she actually began to feel forgiveness. However, the choice came first.

While still in a place before God Himself, after forgiving the person who has hurt or offended us, we need to receive His healing oil into our hearts, as He is the Healer of broken hearts (see Isaiah 61:1–3).

Then, as we pray for and bless the person who wounded us, we will start to develop love in our heart for that person. We are to pursue praying for and blessing even those who position themselves as our enemies (see Matthew 5:43–45).

> We are to pursue praying for and blessing even those who position themselves as our enemies.

Many years ago, I was deeply wounded by someone I had trusted, but who spoke against me to many leaders. After I had examined my own heart, chosen to forgive, and received a degree of healing in my heart, I still woke up with nightmares in which this person was accusing me. I realized the process needed to go deeper, much like peeling off layers of an onion. The Lord led me to pray blessings over that man and his family each day. At first, it was only by obedience, but later, the feelings followed, and I actually began to pity him and to fervently pray for his healing and blessing. Finally, one night I no longer had the nightmare about his accusations, but instead had a dream that we were walking together in a beautiful forest, and speaking with each other as friends.

Although that man never repented to me, and he even lost his family and church as a result of his harsh and judgmental attitudes, when that happened, I did not feel some kind of joy at being "justified". Rather, I experienced deep sorrow that he had missed the beautiful plans God had for his life. And I was able to go on with life without his wounding words continuing to cripple me emotionally.

Second, deal with the spiritual warfare against the relationship. It's important that we allow the Lord to examine our own hearts first, so that we do not fall into the easy trap of blaming everything on the other person, or on demonic attacks against our relationship. However, once we have had cleansing and healing, we reach a more objective place where the Lord can reveal to us any demonic strategies against our relationship. We also are more able to recognize that not everything is *only* our fault, or *only* the fault of the other person.

We recognize that *"our struggle is not against flesh and blood, but against the rulers, against the authorities, against the powers of this dark world and against the spiritual forces of evil in the heavenly realms"* (Ephesians 6:12). We can "bind" in the name of Jesus the demonic forces that have been warring against our relationship. We can tear down through prayer the lies of the enemy that have become mental strongholds in us or in the other person.

We need to "change the channel" on the television of our mind away from the negative, accusatory thoughts toward that person to thoughts that are *"true, noble, just, pure, lovely, of good report—if there is any virtue, and if there is anything praiseworthy—meditate on these things"* (Philippians 4:8).

Changing the Channel

When I was a young pastor around 1980, a couple came to my office for marriage counseling. I had only been married about three years myself, and I felt quite overwhelmed as the man and his wife both started yelling accusations about each other. In my mind, I asked the Lord to quickly give me a word of wisdom. The word of wisdom was: "Be quiet!" To my surprise, they did shut up, and I asked them each to take a paper and pen. I then asked them to each write on their paper five reasons why they had married the other person in the first place. They each sat there in a very defensive posture, arms crossed, and scowling, trying to think of one good thing about their spouse. But once they "changed the channel" from the negative fixation, they then were able to quickly think of five good things about the other person.

Then I asked them to write down five things that *they* had said or done that had wounded their mate. Again, they each sat there in a very defensive posture, arms crossed, and scowling, trying to think of one thing they had ever done wrong. But, once again, when they "changed the channel" from thinking only about the things that they felt justified themselves, they were able to quickly write down the hurtful words or actions they had said or done.

Then I asked them to read their papers to each other. They started weeping and asking forgiveness, and were reconciled by the grace of God. I wish I could say that has always happened in marriage counseling. But unfortunately, some refuse to "change the channel" and admit there are good things about the other person, or bad things they've done that damaged the relationship.

Only then, deal directly with the person involved. After we have allowed the Lord to change and heal our own hearts, and have broken demonic interference and mental strongholds coming against the relationship, we are now ready to approach the person directly.

Building Bridges of Love

A key verse for this step is Ephesians 4:15, which indicates that an aspect of spiritual maturity is *"speaking the truth in love."* One way to picture this verse is to see ourselves building a bridge of love that is strong enough to hold the weight of the truth that needs to be spoken. If you drive a truck loaded with heavy truth onto a very flimsy bridge, you will not be able to deliver that truth.

This became very real to me as a young pastor in the early 1980s. I had "inherited" an elder in the church who had been appointed under the previous pastor. He decided he did not like some of the direction the church was taking, and reports began to come to me of negative criticism of me that he was voicing to some in the church.

By then, I had begun to understand the steps I have shared here, so I asked the Lord, and He showed me where there was some measure of truth in this elder's criticism. I repented of those things, chose to forgive him, received healing in my heart, and started to pray blessing over him daily. I also prayed to bind a spirit of anger that I had discerned working in this man.

As I prayed about when to confront this elder, I felt the Lord say I first needed to "build a bridge of love," which I could do now that my own heart was in a better place. I asked my wife, Patricia, to prepare a special meal for him. Afterwards, we sat in front of the fireplace to have dessert and coffee. I could sense his tension, that he was waiting for me to confront him. Instead, I prayed a sincere blessing over this man and his wife. I felt I should wait until another occasion to confront him. But the next day he called me. He asked forgiveness for speaking against me to others. I said I knew, and had already forgiven him. He then asked me to pray for him, as he realized there was a spirit of anger working in his life, and he needed freedom from it. How amazing it was to see how the Lord had worked to bring restoration. He became my friend after that.

I wish I could say there is such a wonderful ending in every situation. I believe if we sincerely follow the steps I have given here, there will be restoration in most strained relationships.

But what if we follow all these steps, and there is still no breakthrough? Then we commit the other person to the Lord, and seek to keep our own hearts right as we pray blessing upon them. Romans 12:18 says, *"If it is possible, as far as it depends on you, live at peace with everyone."*

I would like to share one more testimony. When I was a pastor in the United States, a man left the church speaking in very negative ways about me. I sought to follow the steps given here, but the man was not open to the healing of our relationship. I forgave him, and left him in the hands of the Lord. About ten years later, while living in Europe, I received a note from this man asking for forgiveness. He explained that he had not left the church because of anything I had done wrong, but because he did not want to face up to a secret sin in his life. Because of that, he felt uncomfortable in our church. After ten years, he decided to repent and wholly follow the Lord. One of the first things the Lord spoke to him was to write and ask my forgiveness for speaking against me in an effort to cover up his sin. The next time I spoke in his city, this man was the first one to run up to me and give me a big hug. He started weeping and saying how much he appreciated me. So even some very difficult situations can be healed as we get our own hearts right, and leave the other person in the hands of the Lord.

Coping With Cross-Cultural Dynamics

Some relational challenges are not due to sin or spiritual warfare, but to cultural or language differences that can cause misunderstandings. Jerusalem lives up to its name as a *"gate to the nations"* (Ezekiel 26:2), so we have a great variety of nationalities and cultures represented at Succat Hallel. And in this day of easy travel, most houses of prayer deal to some degree with cross-cultural dynamics in their relationships. It's therefore important to note that some relational strains need to be understood in this context. If you are a leader in a house of prayer, it may be helpful to do some reading on cross-cultural relationship dynamics.

For example, one culture may place great value on "saving face", so people will be very hesitant to confront, and certainly never in front of others. A contrasting culture may value being very honest and direct, and someone from that culture could deeply wound someone from the "saving face" culture by reprimanding them before others. One culture may value not failing, and therefore be fearful to take risks. A contrasting culture may value pioneering and risk-taking, and as a result would be not so fearful of failure. One culture may be oriented toward long-term planning and preparation, while a contrasting culture may be spontaneous and able to improvise. One culture may emphasize submission to authority and the good of the group, while another feels strongly about independent thinking and judgment. One culture may insist on developing a relationship first before discussing working together, while another forms relationships only after agreeing on the vision and goals.

Rather than judging others over cultural differences, we should seek to listen to and understand one another. We need to speak with each other about recognizing the differing values and approaches of our respective cultures. And we need to give a lot of grace as to how we evaluate the communications and actions of someone from a contrasting culture. An example is given in chapter 2, in the section on apostolic and prophetic input, about how a relational

> **We need to give a lot of grace as to how we evaluate the communications and actions of someone from a contrasting culture.**

strain between two couples from contrasting cultures was healed as their linguistic and cultural misunderstandings were discussed in an atmosphere of love and trust.

The Priority of Godly Love

Ultimately, nothing described in this book really works without love. We must keep as our priority in the house of prayer to "'**love** the Lord your God with all your heart and with all your soul and with all your strength and with all your mind'; and, '**Love** your neighbor as yourself'" (Luke 10:27, emphasis added).

We love the house of prayer because so often, potential relational difficulties are dealt with very early by the Lord speaking to people while they are worshipping Him, showing them to go ask forgiveness of someone, to humble themselves, to serve someone, and other ways to be reconciled.

When I was young, a mentor shared something very valuable with me about cultivating love for one another. He suggested I take 1 Corinthians 13:4–6 and put it in the first person, substituting "I" for the word "love," and then put it on a paper on our refrigerator, or somewhere else I could see it. Then I was to proclaim out loud often: "By the grace of God, I am patient. I am kind. I do not envy, I do not boast, I am not proud. I do not dishonor others, I am not self-seeking, I am not easily angered, I keep no record of wrongs. I do not delight in evil, but rejoice with the truth. I always protect, always trust, always hope, and always persevere." I look back to that small piece of advice as something that had a major effect on my life. Often, when I am tempted to respond in an unloving way, a phrase from that paper rises up within me and says, "I keep no record of wrongs," etc.

May the Lord give us grace to truly love Him with all that is within us, and to love those with us in the house of prayer with His love.

CHAPTER 10

The Power of Thanksgiving

Give thanks to the Lord for He is good; His love endures forever.
—Psalm 118:1

Thanksgiving Transports Us to Realms of Glory

Solomon had the privilege of seeing the manifested glory of God fall during the dedication of the temple, when the musicians and singers joined together as one in a beautiful song of thanks and praise to the Lord for His goodness and love. Giving thanks involves humility and grace. When we give thanks to God in unity with our brothers and sisters, His grace falls upon us and His glory comes.

*13 When the trumpeters and singers were as one, to make one sound to be heard in praising and **thanking** the Lord, and when they lifted up their voice with the trumpets and cymbals and instruments of music, and praised the Lord, saying: "For He is good, for His mercy endures forever," that the house, the house of the Lord, was filled with a cloud, 14 so that the priests could not continue ministering because of the cloud; for the glory of the*

His glory comes through thanking and praising Him in unity with our brothers and sisters, proclaiming He is good.

Lord filled the house of God." (2 Chronicles 5:13–14, NKJV; emphasis added)

We long to see His glory fall in our houses of prayer. His glory comes through thanking and praising Him in unity with our brothers and sisters, proclaiming He is good. He is always good. But it is not always easy to thank and praise Him.

In January of 2016 we received a terrifying phone call from Esther, our youngest daughter, who was then twenty-six years old. She was living in England at the time with her husband and baby boy. She called to say that she had just been diagnosed with Stage 3 triple negative breast cancer. The doctor said her chances of survival were not good. They told her she only had about six months to live, because this particular cancer was so aggressive, especially in young women. Rick and I were devastated. The next day I was praying and asking God about Esther. He said a lot of things, but the main things I remembered were four simple phrases:

"I love Esther.

I want to restore her.

I want to heal her.

Will you praise Me?"

What a challenge He put before me. After hearing that horrible news, He wanted me to praise Him and trust that He wanted to restore and heal her, even when the doctors were not giving me any hope for the future. How could I praise Him before seeing her restored and healed? Just eighteen months before that phone call, I had been in a hospital with Esther hearing the difficult news that her firstborn son, Caleb, had just been diagnosed with Down's syndrome. How much heartache could this young woman, her husband, and we, as her extended family, possibly bear?

Every day since that time, we've had to daily offer a sacrifice of thanksgiving and in this process we have seen the power of thanksgiving. I spent a lot of time these past four years taking care of our special grandson, Caleb. One of the most wonderful things about

Caleb is that he loves to sing! I taught him many Sunday School songs with actions before hearing Esther's diagnosis, like the song "Running Over":

> *Running over, running over*
> *My cup is full and running over*
> *Since the Lord saved me*
> *I'm as happy as can be!*

Many people in Caleb's life taught him different songs, but this became his favorite *"Savta"* song. (*Savta* is the Hebrew word for Grandma) Every time I held Caleb, he would take my hands and do the actions to this song. In this way, he *made* me praise the Lord, even at times when all I wanted to do was scream or cry because of seeing our daughter suffer, or dealing with a bad report from the doctor, or just feeling tired from the everyday battles of cancer.

I started singing out of duty, but the words ministered to me, and I began to sing those words with Caleb in Spirit and in truth. I slowly realized I can be *"as happy as can be since* (or because) *the Lord saved me,"* not because of my circumstances here on earth.

True joy is not found in a happy-go-lucky life. It is found in knowing God.

There is no cancer in heaven. I began to think about eternity and how relatively short this earthly life is. True joy is not found in a happy-go-lucky life. It is found in knowing God. A friend of ours who had gone through very difficult times sent us this quote: "It is better to know God than to know why." This experience has drawn our entire family so much closer to God, as worshipping Him was our only means of getting through many long, difficult days. As we worshipped Him, we were drawn into a higher place of joy and peace—a peace the world can't give, and can't take away.

Our daughter went home to be with the Lord two years and eight months after the cancer diagnosis. Even now I can truly say, "Yes Lord, you are good. You are always good." Even when I don't understand what is happening with my mind, my spirit rises up and says, "God, you are good." Esther's last words to us as we stood around her hospital bed were *"Hodu l'Adonai ki tov,"* a Hebrew scripture, which translated into English says, "Give thanks to the Lord, for He is good." She looked deep into our eyes and said it many times to me, to her dad, to her husband, and even to her doctor, with so much conviction. I praise the Lord that even in her suffering, she was thanking Him for His goodness and exhorting us to do the same.

No matter how difficult the trial we are facing, we can always say to ourselves, "Give thanks to the Lord for He is good, and His love endures forever." It is always true, because He is in control and He is always good. As these words were so alive in Esther before she went home to be with the Lord, we pray that these words would live and vibrate in us every day.

Sometimes we forget to thank the Lord, but through thanksgiving we can overcome bitterness, resentment, and all the lies of the evil one, and find strength to face the future. Thanksgiving changes our focus, softens our hearts, fills us with love, joy, and peace, and lifts our eyes to heaven.

In the Tabernacle of David, the Levites were appointed to stand every morning and every evening to sing thanks and praises to Lord. (See 1 Chronicles 23:30.) **There was even a special minister who was appointed to lead the people in thanksgiving.** In Nehemiah 11:17, we read about *"Mattaniah son of Mika, the son of Zabdi, the son of Asaph, the director who led in thanksgiving and prayer."* It was his *job* to lead in thanksgiving and prayer. Four generations later, Jehaziel, a descendant of Mattaniah, followed in the footsteps of his forefather. Like Mattaniah, he also understood the power of thanksgiving, and he inspired King Jehoshaphat to appoint singers to lead the nation in a powerful song of thanksgiving that protected Israel and led to the defeat of her enemies.

Thanksgiving and Praise Overcome the Enemy

2 Chronicles tells a beautiful thanksgiving story. King Jehoshaphat faced many enemies—"a vast army"—and he called all Judah to

inquire of the Lord for direction. He prayed, *"We do not know what to do, but our eyes are upon You"* (2 Chronicles 20:12). The Spirit of the Lord came upon a Levite—a descendant of Mattaniah (the director of thanksgiving), and He gave the king prophetic direction to deal with this military threat:

14 Then the Spirit of the Lord came upon Jahaziel the son of Zechariah, the son of Benaiah, the son of Jeiel, the son of Mattaniah, a Levite of the sons of Asaph, in the midst of the assembly. 15 He said, Listen, all you of Judah and you inhabitants of Jerusalem, and you, King Jehoshaphat! Thus says the Lord to you: 'Do not be afraid nor dismayed because of this great multitude, for the battle is not yours, but God's. 16 Tomorrow go down against them. They will surely come up by the Ascent of Ziz, and you will find them at the end of the brook before the Wilderness of Jeruel. 17 You will not need to fight in this battle. Position yourselves, stand still and see the salvation of the Lord...

*20 Jehoshaphat stood and said, "Listen to me, Judah and people of Jerusalem! Have faith in the Lord your God and you will be upheld; have faith in His prophets and you will be successful." 21 After consulting the people, Jehoshaphat appointed men to sing to the Lord and to praise Him for the splendor of His holiness as they went out at the head of the army, saying: "**Give thanks to the Lord, for His love endures forever**." 22 As they began to sing and praise, the Lord set ambushes against the men of Ammon and Moab and Mount Seir who were invading Judah, and they were defeated.*

23 The Ammonites and Moabites rose up against the men from Mount Seir to destroy and annihilate them. After they finished slaughtering the men from Seir, they helped to destroy one another. 24 When the men of Judah came to the place that overlooks the desert and looked toward the vast army, they saw only dead bodies lying on the ground; no one had escaped. 25 So Jehoshaphat and his men went to carry off their plunder, and they found among them a great amount of equipment and clothing and also articles of value—more than they could take away. There was so much plunder that it took three days to collect it. 26 On the fourth day they assembled in the Valley of Berakah, where they praised the Lord ... 27 Then, led by Jehoshaphat, all the men of Judah and Jerusalem returned joyfully to Jerusalem, for the Lord had given them cause to rejoice over their enemies. 28 They entered Jerusalem and went to the temple of the Lord with harps and lyres and trumpets. 29 The fear of God came on all the surrounding kingdoms when they heard how the Lord had fought against the enemies of Israel. 30 And the kingdom of Jehoshaphat was at peace, for his God had given him rest on every side (NKJV; emphasis added).

Thanksgiving Honors the Lord

Psalm 50:23 (AMP) says, *"He who offers a sacrifice of praise and thanksgiving honors Me; and to him who orders his way rightly [who follows the way that I show him], I shall show the salvation of God."*

> Thanksgiving is the most terrifying thing imaginable to the enemy of our souls.

Much of the time thanksgiving is a sacrifice. I'm sure it wasn't easy to be part of the choir in the days of Jehoshaphat! To stand in front of those hateful armies and sing a song of thanks doesn't seem logical. Nor does it seem very threatening to the enemy! But thanksgiving is the most terrifying thing imaginable to the enemy of our souls. He can't get to us when we are thankful. None of his tactics work. Self-pity, bitterness, doubt and unbelief have to flee before a thankful heart. All of us face many challenges, and it is so easy to focus on our challenges or disappointments. But we were made to praise him, so when we begin our day and our worship watches with thanks, we order our way rightly and we give no place to the enemy.

One of my favorite chapters in the Bible is Psalm 100:

A Psalm of Thanksgiving

1 Make a joyful shout to the Lord all you lands!

2 Serve the Lord with gladness;

Come before His presence with singing.

3 Know that the Lord, He is God;

It is He who has made us, and not we ourselves;

We are His people and the sheep of His pasture.

4 Enter into His gates with thanksgiving,

And into His courts with praise.

Be thankful to Him and bless His name.

5 For the Lord is good; His mercy is everlasting,

And His truth endures to all generations. (NKJV)

My second-grade teacher had me memorize this psalm, and I have such good memories of her because of this. I am forever grateful to her for requiring our class to memorize scripture, as we retain what we learn as children so much more than what we retain as adults. It makes me want to work with children and teach them to memorize scripture! Here I am fifty-five years later, and my entire life's work has been seeking to fulfill and to facilitate others to fulfill this scripture. It is my joy to lead watches and to schedule others to lead watches. Succat Hallel (Hebrew for "Tent of Praise") is so aptly the name of our 24/7 house of praise, worship and prayer. I was made to praise Him, and I'm so thankful He has allowed us to build a dwelling place for Him, where He is worshipped and praised twenty-four hours a day, seven days a week.

Psalm 100:4 says: *"Enter into His gates with thanksgiving and into His courts with praise. Be thankful unto Him and bless His name."* What does it mean to enter His gates? His gates are the entrance into His presence. So how can we feel his presence? Thank Him!

When I begin a worship watch with a thankful heart and sing songs of thanksgiving and praise, I feel the favor of the Lord and I am carried by His presence. Time flies because the wind of His Spirit catches me up into an eternal realm where time does not exist—only eternal rapture and delight. After leading a worship time like this, I am usually exhilarated and not tired at all. Thanksgiving is how we as a community have been able to maintain 24/7 worship and prayer for over fifteen years without getting burnt out.

> A thankful heart prepares the way of the Lord. It's the red carpet for the King of Kings.

Thanksgiving honors the King and puts Him first. In the book of Esther, many times Esther asked the question, "What would please the King?" She was attractive to the king, and she was chosen to be queen because of her attitude of humility and her desire to please him. She was centered upon him and not upon herself. This was beautiful in his eyes. So if we want to please the King, the Word of God says that thanksgiving and praise honor Him, and it is comely (beautiful, fitting,) for the upright (see Psalm 33:1). Sometimes after a great time of thanks and praise, I look in the mirror and I do a double take because the glory is still on my face and I look ten years younger!

This is the proper way to come before the King of Kings—to honor Him with a thankful heart. Thanksgiving is the protocol we need to follow in coming before Him. It brings salvation and blessing to our lives and our times of worship. A thankful heart prepares the way of the Lord. It's the red carpet for the King of Kings.

Thanksgiving Transforms Us

Because His courts are filled with praise—doubt, unbelief, and unforgiveness are left at the door, for we can't be truly thankful and still have negative thoughts and feelings. Thanksgiving lifts us into a different realm—the realm of the Spirit! It's the doorway to the heavenly places. I want to live there! We experience love, joy, peace, kindness, goodness, faithfulness, patience, humility, and self-control when we give thanks (see Galatians 5:22). All these wonderful fruits of the Spirit rush into our beings when we simply say "thank you" and our minds are renewed, our spirits lifted, and our bodies healed. Praise is so good for us! *"It is good to praise the Lord and make music to Your Name, O Most High"* (Psalm 92:1).

I hear Psalm 100:4 (NKJV)—*"Be thankful to Him and bless His name"*—fulfilled almost every day in Israel. In Hebrew, *Barukh ha Shem* means "Blessed be the Name." Israelis say, *"Barukh ha Shem"* in response to the question "How are you?" This has been an example for me. No matter what we are going through, it is always appropriate to say, "Bless His name." Even if I'm having a hard day, I bless His Name. I love living in a land where the normal response for "How are you?" is *"Barukh ha Shem"*—Blessed be the Name!

Thanksgiving Releases Love

Sometimes we don't understand other people or how their actions affect us, but the Lord wants to order our way rightly toward them, and thanking Him accomplishes that. As we thank the Lord for them and trust that He has everything and everyone under His control, it causes us to pray with love, and focus on their good points.

Thanksgiving Releases Blessing

Thanksgiving is like a bomb going off inside of us—it explodes the lies of the enemy and breaks off curses. It reminds me of a scene from a movie when everything is under a curse, and darkness and heaviness cover the land, but when the curse is broken, everything comes alive with sparkling light.

I see the inside of us like a world either covered in darkness or covered in light. Thanksgiving turns that light on. It takes us from darkness to light, sadness to joy, despair to hope, anguish to peace, bondage to freedom, boredom to exhilaration, and death to life. Through thanksgiving, our world comes alive—vision is released, and prayers answered.

One of our former watch leaders, Stevenson Simplice, once had a vision about thanksgiving. He saw the prayers of many saints forming above in the heavens like clouds. But the rains of blessing were not coming down upon the people who were not giving thanks. Those who gave thanks were rained upon with blessings and answers to their prayers. Those who thanked the Lord even received the blessings of the intercession of others who had not received answers to their prayers because of unthankful hearts.

Oh Lord, forgive us when we forget to thank You. Help us to encourage others to be thankful, and overwhelm us with Your glory as we learn to thank You together with one voice and one heart.

CHAPTER 11

A Prophetic Flow of Praise, Worship, and Prayer

Each one had a harp and they were holding golden bowls full of incense, which are the prayers of God's people.
And they sang a new song.

—Revelation 5:8–9

In the first "house of prayer" (the Tabernacle of David and the Temple worship) David and his musicians placed a great priority on the prophetic, and made room for it in their watches. In a sense, David planned for the unplanned, making a place for, and providing supervision and training for spontaneous prophecy to happen.

1 Chronicles 25:1–3 states:

1 David, together with the commanders of the army, set apart some of the sons of Asaph, Heman and Jeduthun for the ministry of prophesying, accompanied by harps, lyres and cymbals. Here is the list of the men who performed this service: 2 From the sons of Asaph: Zakkur, Joseph, Nethaniah and Asarelah. The sons of Asaph were under the supervision of Asaph, who prophesied under the king's supervision. 3 As for Jeduthun, from his sons: Gedaliah, Zeri, Jeshaiah, Shimei, Hashabiah and Mattithiah, six in all, under the supervision of their father Jeduthun, who prophesied, using the harp in thanking and praising the Lord.

The Psalms are mostly a record of what took place in the Tabernacle of David, as the king appointed certain Levites to record its activities. So certain occurrences in the Psalms make more sense if we understand them as records of what was happening in watches of praise, worship and intercession. For example, Psalm 95 flows from a time of joyful praise and thanksgiving (verses 1–5), to a time of bowing and kneeling before the Lord in worship (verses 6–7), to a time of the Lord speaking through prophecy to His people (verses 8–11):

1 Come, let us sing for joy to the LORD;
let us shout aloud to the Rock of our salvation.
2 Let us come before Him with thanksgiving
and extol Him with music and song.

3 For the LORD is the great God,
the great King above all gods.
4 In His hand are the depths of the earth,
and the mountain peaks belong to Him.
5 The sea is His, for He made it,
and His hands formed the dry land.

6 Come, let us bow down in worship,
let us kneel before the LORD our Maker;
7 for He is our God
and we are the people of His pasture,
the flock under His care.

Today, if only you would hear His voice,
8 Do not harden your hearts as you did at Meribah,
as you did that day at Massah in the wilderness,
9 where your ancestors tested Me;
they tried Me, though they had seen what I did.
10 For forty years I was angry with that generation;
I said, "They are a people whose hearts go astray,
and they have not known My ways."
11 So I declared on oath in My anger,
'They shall never enter My rest.'"

Making Room for the Prophetic

We believe it is important to make room for a flow of the prophetic in watches, which will generate prayer and proclamation based on hearing what the Lord is saying to us at that moment.

Start at the Throne of God

Rather than coming to a watch with our own agenda for prayer, we need to start at His throne. To approach a king, it is important to follow the protocol for entering the presence of that king. And the King of Kings has issued a protocol for approaching Him, which is to *"enter His gates with thanksgiving and His courts with praise; give thanks to Him and praise His name"* (Psalm 100:4). In Psalm 95, cited above, that time of prayer and worship started with thanksgiving and praise. Praise is not necessarily a fast tempo or a particular style of music, but rather, it is acknowledging God's mighty acts and perfect character.

> Rather than coming to a watch with our own agenda for prayer, we need to start at His throne.

Praise Flows into Worship

It's natural for praise to flow into worship, where we fall before Him in awe, and respond to His heart by "ascribing worth" to Him and pouring out our love upon Him.

David described his heart for worship this way: *"One thing I ask from the Lord, this only do I seek: that I may dwell in the house of the Lord all the days of my life, to gaze on the beauty of the Lord and to seek Him in His temple"* (Psalm 27:4).

Another way to say, "seek Him" is to "pursue Him". When a young man pursues a young woman to become his wife, part of that pursuing is not just to talk about her, but also to listen to her, to seek to know her as she really is, to seek to know her heart.

> It is natural in a place of worship intimacy to hear what the Lord is whispering, and to feel what He is feeling.

As we seek Him in prophetic worship, we draw closer in intimacy to sense His heart and listen to Him. It is natural in a place of worship intimacy to hear what the Lord is whispering, and to feel what He is feeling. Often when a musician plays a spontaneous song that is more than music, it actually enables us to feel something the Lord Himself is feeling. Sometimes prophetic music releases someone to sing a prophetic song, or to declare a spontaneous prophetic declaration that interprets what was played musically.

However, not everything spontaneous is prophetic. In praise and worship times, there also may be musical interludes, or "jamming". These can be great blessings, but are not necessarily prophetic. In my understanding, we are prophetic when we communicate or release the Lord's thoughts or feelings. A strong example is the prophecies of Hosea, in which he experiences through the unfaithfulness of his wife the suffering in the Lord's heart over Israel's unfaithfulness to Him.

Worship Releases Holy Spirit Revelation

King David is considered one of the greatest military commanders in history. Yet one of his main methods of gathering military intelligence would be considered foolish by most military leaders today: he appointed prophetic musicians to play until the Holy Spirit released prophetic revelation, as mentioned above in the reference to 1 Chronicles 25:1–3.

Although it is not wrong to pray in response to the news or our understanding of a situation, the Lord is increasingly releasing the anointing to cause us to rise up into His perspective from the third heaven (see 2 Corinthians 12:2–4). There things are revealed to us that we cannot possibly know by our natural mind. In these inspired moments, we receive revelation—including revelation that may require governmental intercession—that is not in *response* to the news, but actually *creates* future headlines together with the Sovereign Lord.

Prophetic Revelation That Led to Military Victory

The combination of prophetic music with prophetic, third-heaven seeing and hearing is described in 2 Kings 3. King Jehoshaphat had joined the kings of Israel and Edom to attack the rebellious king of Moab. But their armies wandered in confusion for seven days and they found themselves in a place with no water for them or their animals. Defeat looked certain. But King Jehoshaphat went to Elisha seeking prophetic direction. He needed more than a prayer based on the situation alone.

It is important to note that Elisha did not start prophesying right off the bat. He recognized his need to enter a place of "third heaven" revelation through prophetic worship. So he said in verse 15a: *"But now bring me a minstrel."* He called for an anointed worship musician, in this case a harpist. Then,

> 15b **it came about, when the minstrel played, that the hand of the** LORD **came upon him**. 16 He said, '**Thus says the** LORD, '**Make this valley full of trenches**.' 17 For thus says the LORD, 'You shall not see wind nor shall you see rain; yet that valley shall be filled with water, so that you shall drink, both you and your cattle and your beasts. 18 This is but a slight thing in the sight of the LORD; He will also give the Moabites into your hand. 19 Then you shall strike every fortified city and every choice city, and fell every good tree and stop all springs of water, and mar every good piece of land with stones.' 20 It happened about the time of offering the morning sacrifice, that behold, water came by the way of Edom, and the country was filled with water (2 Kings 3:15–20, NASB; emphasis added).

As an anointed musician played, Elisha saw and heard a clear military strategy and a miraculous intervention that would lead to victory for King Jehoshaphat and those allied with him.

A Modern-day Example

By God's grace, we've often seen a release of prophetic revelation during worship watches in Succat Hallel, but I'd like to share one illustration with you, a vision I received during worship:

On 24 March 2009, I saw a map of Israel like a steak, a piece of fresh meat. Then I saw witches and warlocks gathering around her northern, eastern, and southern borders. Next, I saw wolves gathering on the hills to the north and the east of Israel. The wolves seemed to be coming especially from Russia and Iran. They began howling and baring their teeth, as if preparing to devour Israel.

Then sharks began swimming from the Black Sea, and gathered along the western coast of Israel and Gaza. The sharks were also baring their teeth as if ready to attack Israel. I remember remarking that there did not seem to be the same level of threat on the southern border (with Egypt) as on the northern, eastern, and western borders. I also remarked that I had not thought before of the seacoast as a border needing to be protected in prayer.

As intercessors in the vision cried out to the Lord to protect Israel, I saw angels flying with shofars, from which they poured out the blood of the Lamb on all the borders of Israel. The blood rose up like a huge red wall, outlining all the borders. Then the witches and warlocks began throwing their potions and witchcraft at Israel, but they all just hit this wall of blood, and ran down it without penetrating the Land. Both the wolves and the sharks drew back a little from the borders. Then I saw a clock indicating five minutes before midnight. The hands on the clock were turned back to ten minutes before midnight.

The next day, 25 March, a messianic pastor who had been in the meeting the night before and heard me describe this vision, called me with great excitement in his voice. He said: "They reported in the news this morning that thirty sharks were caught off the coast of Israel near Ashdod. I never heard of more than one shark in all my years here, but they said this group of thirty sharks had swum in as a menace off the coast. But they caught them all, and the coast is now safe again."

I understood this as a confirming sign in the natural, but sensed there was still more that the Lord sought to communicate in this vision.

On 26 March, I received the second part of the vision. As intercessors continued to cry out for the protection of Israel, I saw huge angels standing on the borders of Israel facing outward and blowing silver trumpets. Then the witches and warlocks began to shrink back, away from the borders. The wolves began running in fear back toward Russia and Iran. The sharks swam away in the direction of the Atlantic Ocean. I then saw the hands on the clock moved back to fifteen minutes before midnight.

Soon after sharing this vision more broadly, I mentioned it to a friend who works in the highest levels of military intelligence and security. He is a man who prays and who believes in prophetic revelation. He told me: "I cannot tell you all I know, because it is classified information, but this vision is from God, and you need to keep praying according to what you have been shown."

Later this man said: "I can now explain more about what you saw in the shark vision, as the information is now declassified and public. We knew the North Koreans had developed a new type of small submarine, almost impossible to track in the waters with existing technology. That's how they were able to surprise a South Korean naval vessel and shoot a torpedo into its side. The name of this North Korean submarine is "The Shark"! At the time that you received a vision about sharks off of the coast of Israel, we already knew that North Korea had sold The Shark to Iran, and we have reason to believe they have also sold it to Syria.[2]

As a result of that vision, we began to pray for the protection of the sea border of Israel in the same way we had prayed until then for the land borders.

Praise God that anointed, prophetic worship can bring us to a place where the Lord can reveal to us subjects for prayer and proclamations that we could not have known with only our natural understanding!

---

2 For those interested, this has now been made public by articles such as *"Submarines: North Korea Builds a Better Shark."* Strategy Page, The News as History. April 16, 2013. (Archives, 2013). https://www.strategypage.com/htmw/htsub/20130416.aspx (accessed April 20, 2013).

Prophetic Proclamation

Sometimes the Lord leads us to prophetic, governmental proclamations. When we receive a third-heaven revelation while waiting on the Lord in worship, often this should be prayed not as a request, but as a proclamation. A good example of this happened to some of our young leaders during a worship watch at Succat Hallel in December 2013. They felt the Lord warned them of a dangerous terror plot that needed to be exposed in our Jerusalem neighborhood, Abu Tor. They proclaimed that the Lord would expose and cut off any terror plot coming from our neighborhood. It was later reported that on 25 December, Shin Bet, the Israel Security Agency, arrested three operatives, one of whom lived in Abu Tor. They were part of an Al-Qaida plan to bomb a Jewish apartment building in our neighborhood, as well as larger targets such as the International Convention Center of Jerusalem, along with the U.S. Embassy, then in Tel Aviv.

We will discuss proclamation prayer in more detail in chapter 14, "The Crown and Throne Paradigm," but here we present it as part of the prophetic flow in a watch.

Contending for a Proclamation With High Praises

There are times in a prophetic flow that the Holy Spirit will lead us into strong, sometimes almost violent praise, battling for what we have just proclaimed. This is scriptural, and was clearly normal in the Tabernacle of David, as evidenced in Psalm 149:

1 Praise the Lord!

Sing to the Lord a new song,

And His praise in the congregation of the godly ones.

2 Let Israel be glad in his Maker;

Let the sons of Zion rejoice in their King.

3 Let them praise His name with dancing;

Let them sing praises to Him with timbrel and lyre.

4 For the Lord takes pleasure in His people;

He will beautify the afflicted ones with salvation.

5 Let the godly ones exult in glory;

Let them sing for joy on their beds.

6 Let the high praises of God be in their mouth,

And a two-edged sword in their hand,

7 To execute vengeance on the nations

And punishment on the peoples,

8 To bind their kings with chains

And their nobles with fetters of iron,

9 To execute on them the judgment written;

This is an honor for all His godly ones.

Praise the Lord! (NASB)

In Psalm 149, the *"high praises"* are characterized by: spontaneous singing of praises (verse 1); great confidence in God expressed by joy (verse 2); physical expressions, including dancing and rhythmic instruments, such as the tambourine and lyre (verse 3).

The results of these *"high praises"* in Psalm 149 are:

(1) The Lord is moved to pleasure, and brings salvation (deliverance) to us, His *"afflicted ones"* (verse 4)

(2) He pours His glory (manifested Presence) and joy upon us (verse 5)

(3) As these "high praises" are in our mouths, and the *"two-edged sword"* (the scriptures) in our hands, we administrate or execute His judgments upon the nations and their governmental leaders (both natural and spiritual), as seen in verses 7–9. We can only carry out those judgments that He has already declared, but our administration of these is effective in changing the nations, and it is an honor for us!

Stay Centered on Him

We conclude our watches with worship to stay centered on God Himself. Even though by His grace, we may have effectively dealt with demonic powers and their strategies, we are not centered on high praise, prayer warfare, or prophecy, but we remain centered on God Himself. *"For from Him, and through Him, and to Him are all things"* (Romans 11:36).

> Too many believers know only the Jesus (Yeshua) revealed in the Gospels, but not the Jesus (Yeshua) revealed in the book of Revelation.

We should never be impressed with the greatness of the enemy, but solely with the greatness of our God. So it is key in this type of prophetic worship to end our time with our eyes and our hearts fixed on Him.

Too many believers know only the Jesus (Yeshua) revealed in the Gospels, but not the Jesus (Yeshua) revealed in the book of Revelation. He is revealed in the book of Revelation as a Man of War, the Lion of Judah, Who rules with power over the nations. Yet He is also the Lamb who is standing *"at the center of the throne"* (Revelation 5:6).

We need to start at His throne, and end at His throne!

PART 2

MANDATES THAT SHIFT NATIONS

CHAPTER 12

Mandates Shape Your Identity

Write the vision and make it plain … that he may run who reads it.
—Habakkuk 2:2 (NKJV)

We were amazed how quickly the Lord brought worship leaders to us when we opened up our living room for public worship. All the leaders the Lord sent to us came with a burning desire and true call for 24/7 worship. We had to learn to appreciate our different streams and styles of worship. We quickly learned how much we needed one another and how beautiful is the Body of Christ. We represented slightly different streams, yet all of us were united in our mandate to hear the Lord's voice, value the leading of the Holy Spirit, pray without ceasing, and worship extravagantly the One who is worthy. But we needed to know whether we were called to somehow combine all of the models that had influenced us, or to require all to conform to only one model.

The Lord had spoken to Patricia and me that, as the "father and mother" of the work, we were to have many different styles and cultures in the watches of Succat Hallel. We really prayed the Lord would show us if we were hearing from Him correctly. The Lord gave us His answer during a visit I made to Kansas City in December 2004. I saw a friend, Jill Austin, who has now gone home to the Lord, and who had a very strong prophetic anointing on her life. At that time, she was officially based out of the International House of Prayer in Kansas City.

Jill invited me and our daughter Esther for coffee. As we were drinking our coffee, Jill's prophetic anointing kicked in, and I was glad I could record what she said. Here is part of it:

Joseph's Coat of Many Colors

"Here [in Kansas City] they've got the bridal. That's very important, the intimacy of the bridal chamber. It's another part of what God has connected you to. You guys being in the heart [Jerusalem], you're connected to different kinds of prayer movements, different streams. So you're part of the strategic militant warfare like Lou Engle, but you're also connected to the governmental like Dutch Sheets and Chuck Pierce, but also to Mike Bickle and the bridal ... All these other guys ... are all pieces [of the puzzle], and there are lots of pieces.

You guys are going to be this living organism, this living artery of His heart, and you can't nail it down—He's not going to let you nail it down. Part of it is that creative thing. You want the wind—the wind and the breath of God on this, because it keeps you dependent, it keeps you humble, and it keeps you for the sovereignty. You need sovereignty. You need miracles, and man and intellect can't give you miracles. You can couple with God, and God has you in this place of partnering with the Holy Spirit to save lives, to go in and rescue lives literally. You guys are called on the front war lines. It's kind of wonderful ... with the House of Prayer [Kansas City], they will come in and say, 'This is what it looks like, this is how you do it.' *Everyone will come in and try and put their pattern over you, even though they say they won't* ... The Lord isn't calling you to be little Mike Bickles or Chuck Pierces, or whatever. *There's a DNA of you guys that's like a Joseph's mantle of all these different colors, and the Holy Spirit pulls on them depending on the crises in the land, and what He's calling you to do.*"

By the Lord's grace, through Jill, the Lord not only answered this question, but her prophetic word gave us even more understanding as to why the Lord had sent us leaders from so many different streams and backgrounds. I felt strongly that He had led us all together, despite the challenge to understand how it was all going to work. But now we had a clear picture that the Lord was piecing us together into a "coat of many colors"—like that of Joseph.

As I prayed, the Lord made it clear that each of these leaders was not just to be released, but also to be encouraged to lead in their very different styles and anointings. One of the young leaders who had been so influenced by Kansas City was sent to us by the Lord to bring in their particular "harp and bowl" and "bridal paradigm" anointing. But another leader, who had mentored under Chuck Pierce, was to bring in that particular prophetic anointing. Patricia and I were to bring the governmental anointing we had been operating in through our "Pray for the City" concerts of prayer and other initiatives.

> The diverse ethnicities the Lord brings to Succat Hallel also impart a variety of anointings.

The Beauty of Diversity

The diverse ethnicities the Lord brings to Succat Hallel also impart a variety of anointings. I see the beauty of ethnic giftings in our house of prayer in Jerusalem, as groups come from many different nations to pray and worship.

When a Chinese group comes, they almost always pray with an anointing for weeping, travailing, birthing prayer. And they have a great love for beauty and art in worship. Many times, they bring beautiful paintings or silks to present to the Lord in worship. They are the only ethnic group I have witnessed holding up large flowers to give to their Bridegroom as they dance!

Almost every time an African group is here, I find them in a place of high praise, with beautiful harmonies, sometimes playing all the drums in the place and dancing with joy to the Lord. It helps to break through the heavy, religious atmosphere so prevalent in Jerusalem.

When Koreans come into the room, they often have an anointing in breakthrough prayer that I call "machine gun prayer". They all pray out loud in tongues at the same time (including groups from almost every denomination).

Once we needed a breakthrough to get permits for the Palestinian young people wanting to come from places like Bethlehem or Ramallah to our youth conference, ELAV. We normally could get these permits

> Each ethnic group has its own distinctive gifts and anointings to bring worship and prayer to the King.

without too much trouble, but that year the Israeli official who usually helped us was away on vacation, and the permits were denied. I asked a Korean group doing a watch at Succat Hallel to pray. They all prayed very loudly and forcefully in tongues, and then they all stopped at the same time, and said it was "accomplished". I found out a day later that the permits had been granted miraculously at almost the exact time these Korean intercessors said it was "accomplished". The Israeli official who was away on vacation called our Palestinian pastor friend and said, "I'm on vacation, but felt impressed I should call you to see if perhaps you need my help for something." Our Palestinian pastor friend explained the situation, and said he had not wanted to disturb the Israeli official. In a few minutes, the Israeli official called back to say we had the permits!

When a French group comes into the room, they often sing beautiful love songs to their Bridegroom, and pray that their worship and prayer will be like a "perfume" unto the Lord. In fact, in France, a house of prayer is commonly called a "house of perfumes"!

I could describe others, but I think you can see how each ethnic group has its own distinctive gifts and anointings to bring worship and prayer to the King.

Eight Mandates Define Succat Hallel's Identity

Mandate No. 1—Restoration of the Tabernacle of David: To pray for and build toward the restoration of the Tabernacle of David, as prophesied in Amos 9:11 and Acts 15:16–18. This means helping to establish 24/7 worship and prayer, not only in Jerusalem, but also in the Middle East. It also means praying toward the Temple Mount, believing for the establishment and restoration of the Throne of David for the Son of David on His Holy Hill in Jerusalem.

Mandate No. 2—Youth Revival in Israel (see Joel 2:28): To serve and minister to the youth; to have a vision for and release youth into the house of prayer, and to believe that this will grow into a prayer movement to help birth a great move of the Holy Spirit among the youth of our nation and region.

Mandate No. 3—Reconciliation and Unity of the Body (see Ephesians 2:14–15): To pray for and encourage unity in the Body of Messiah (Christ) in Israel between Jewish messianic, Arab, and international believers. We feel the Lord has strongly called us to pray for and encourage the working together of the *"one new man,"* Jew and Gentile.

Mandate No. 4—The Isaiah 19 Highway and Multiplication of Houses of Prayer in the Region (Isaiah 19:23–25): To pray for the establishment and realization of a highway of worship and reconciliation over the Isaiah 19 region, which includes most of the Middle East, Israel, and Egypt.

Mandate No. 5—Comfort His People, Israel, to Prepare the Way of the Lord: Isaiah 40 exhorts us to "comfort" Zion, to receive the Lord's heart for the Jewish people, and to pray for Israel.

Mandate No. 6—The Jeremiah 31:38–40 Watch: To watch over the specific geographical area that includes Mount Zion, the Temple Mount, the City of David, the Ben Hinnom Valley, and the hilltops of the tribe of Judah facing Mount Zion and the Temple Mount. This doesn't mean that others could not also be called to watch over some of that area, but that the Lord has sovereignly positioned us there, and we are to take strong, serious responsibility to watch over that area of Jerusalem.

Mandate No. 7—Making Room for the Work of the Holy Spirit Through the Prophetic and Healing. As we are facing Mount Zion and the traditional site of the Upper Room, we desire to see a new outpouring of the Holy Spirit that would release the prophetic. And with Acts 10:38 as a model, we are called to press in to God for reopening the well of the healing ministry of Yeshua (Jesus) in Jerusalem. We believe that an outpouring of healing signs and wonders is key for what the Lord wants to do in Jerusalem, Israel, and the Middle East.

Mandate No. 8—Intercession for Government and the other "Mountains of Society". We are called in a special way to "watch" over government, but also to watch over other "mountains of society," such as media, arts and entertainment, education, business, the family, and religion.

Identifying the Calling of a House of Prayer

Recognizing the different kinds of houses of prayer that the Lord has raised up will clarify your house of prayer's calling. Just as each child in a family is unique, so are the various models for houses of prayer. It is important in the birthing phase to hear from the Lord the type of house of prayer He desires to establish through you. Here are some possible models of a house of prayer we have identified:

The 24/7 House of Prayer

This model is based on the scriptures that indicate the Tabernacle (or Tent) of David was a place of 24/7 worship and intercession. 1 Chronicles 16:37 says that David *"left Asaph and his relatives before the ark of the covenant of the LORD to minister before the ark **continually**, as every day's work required"* (NASB, emphasis added). This same Hebrew word, *tamid*, is used in Leviticus 6:13 to say that the fire on the altar in the Tabernacle of Moses *"must be kept burning on the altar **continuously**; it must not go out."* The fact that the worship and prayer in the Tabernacle of David was 24/7 is further underpinned by the sheer number of David's Levitical musicians—four thousand—mentioned in 1 Chronicles 23:5. That is not a small worship team— it was more than enough to cover twenty-four hours of worship, seven days a week.

> When the Lord calls you to 24/7 worship and prayer, He will raise up and send in the watchmen and women who are needed to fulfill that call.

From the beginning of our call, the Lord indicated that Succat Hallel was to become 24/7 when He gave us a foundational scripture, Isaiah 62:6–7: "*I have posted watchmen on your walls, Jerusalem; they will never be silent day or night. You who call on the LORD, give yourselves no rest, and give Him no rest till He establishes Jerusalem and makes her the praise of the earth.*"

In many situations, it is practically impossible, and in others, that vision can become a heavy yoke if it is not the calling of the Lord. We found from experience that when the Lord calls you to 24/7 worship and prayer, He will raise up and send in the watchmen and women who are needed to fulfill that call.

The Citywide, Inter-Congregational House of Prayer

Some houses of prayer are not called to be identified as the "prayer room" or "prayer ministry" of only one church or congregation. They are perceived as more of a neutral hub of prayer involving worshipers and intercessors from across their city. Succat Hallel has this calling, and as a result, we have raised up and provided worship leaders, musicians, intercessors, and youth leaders for different congregations in Jerusalem. As they have seen that we have a heart to serve them in that way, they have felt free to release their members to be involved in Succat Hallel, and often have told us that their people were an even greater blessing to their local congregations afterward because of what they experienced at Succat Hallel.

The Local Church Prayer Room or House of Prayer

Others are led to have a prayer room or house of prayer that is clearly identified as the ministry of one church or congregation, though it may also be open to those from other congregations. Often, one of their major mandates is to pray for the vision and needs of that local congregation. In our experience, it is often more difficult, though not impossible, to establish a 24/7 house of prayer using this model. Most local congregations do not have the resources to staff 24/7. However, in some nations that are experiencing extraordinary growth of the Body (such as Indonesia), we have seen a local congregation able to staff 24/7. Again, the most important factor is determining whether this is a clear word from the Lord.

The Live-In Community House of Prayer

In 1987, before we came to Jerusalem, our friend Tom Hess was led to found Jerusalem House of Prayer for All Nations on the Mount of Olives. He knew his mandate had to do with preparing for the King of Glory's return to the Mount of Olives, and to be a global, 24/7 house of prayer for Israel and the nations. The core prayer and worship is carried out by staff from many nations who live together in community, joined by guests from all over Israel and from the nations, who stay in the guesthouse or visit for the day. They have since founded two other live-in community, 24/7, harp and bowl[3] houses of prayer—in Eilat, on the southernmost border of Israel, and the Mount Herman Golan house of prayer in the north.

In 2006, the Lord raised up The City of David Prayer Room, associated with Succat Hallel, which is primarily a live-in community. John and Una Gere had moved into the City of David around the same time we started Succat Hallel. They came to our first public watch, and shortly after that became part of the leadership team. In 2006, the Lord led Steve and Tonya Hansen, the leaders of our first internship program, to move into the City of David compound. After a time, they felt they should step out in faith to ask the owner of the compound if he would rent us a large room to use as a prayer room. Shortly after that, the Hansens had to go back to the United States, and John and Una have faithfully led this community and prayer room for many years. Intercessors have lived there in community to keep a flame of worship and prayer going in this very strategic location just under the Temple Mount, very close to—and possibly even on—the location of the original Tabernacle of David.

The 'Guesthouse' House of Prayer

The guesthouse model receives intercessors and worshippers coming to pray for a city or nation. Gwen Shaw, founder of a movement called the End-time Handmaidens and Servants of the Lord, had

---

3   Please see English Glossary

established such a ministry in Jerusalem before we came. That ministry graciously allowed us to hold several watches a week in their facility for about three years before the Lord gave us our own place.

Their guesthouse, The House of Peace, continues to receive intercessors from their movement who come from many nations to pray around Israel and in Jerusalem. One of their mandates is to facilitate "on-site, prophetic prayer assignments" throughout Israel. They also have at least one weekly prayer meeting in the House of Peace.

Succat Hallel oversaw a guesthouse in Jericho for a time where guests used to come for a day or several days in order to pray in this strategic eastern gate of Israel.

The 'Place of Refuge' House of Prayer

As we have travelled in the nations, we have increasingly encountered houses of prayer whose main mandate is to prepare a "place of refuge." One such prayer center in Egypt came about through a vision received by an Egyptian leader well before the major shakings of that nation started with the Arab Spring of 2011. They found an oasis in the desert where they established a small farm and built housing to take care of believers in times of strong persecution. Patricia and I had the privilege of travelling there with some Israeli Messianic Jewish leaders, who, together with several of our Egyptian friends, laid a foundation stone for this place of refuge. A Bible, opened to the promises of Isaiah 19, which prophesies great shakings followed by a great turning to the Lord in Egypt, was laid in the foundations of this altar. Soon after that, Egypt started to experience a first wave of shakings, confirming the need for refuge houses of prayer.

In certain places of the world with large Jewish populations, I have met many people called to help establish a "place of refuge" house of prayer for Jews who will need refuge as they flee violent anti-Semitism. These different people were totally unaware that the Lord was calling many others besides themselves to the same vision. They currently meet with other believers to pray for the Jewish people according to Jeremiah 16:16—"'But now I will send for many fishermen,' declares the Lord, 'and they will catch them. After that I will send for many *hunters, and they will hunt them down on every mountain and hill and from the crevices of the rocks.'"*

These groups pray that the Jewish people will hear the Lord's command to return to the Land of Israel while it is still the time of the "fishermen", when they can return with their families and finances intact. But these "place of refuge" intercessors are also preparing places in which to hide Jews along an "underground railroad" to aid them in fleeing back to Israel in the time of the "hunters" [a time of great and violent anti-Semitism].

The 'Apostolic Hub' House of Prayer

This house of prayer is called to become a center of training and sending people forth to help establish other houses of prayer in a nation, region, or nations. Usually these are 24/7 houses of prayer that have a strong core of leadership raised up by the Lord. An obvious example is the International House of Prayer in Kansas City.

Here in the Middle East, I had a vision of several such "apostolic hubs" being raised up. They had revolving doors, with people continually being sent in for training, and being sent out into the region to help birth and encourage new houses of prayer.

The Blending of Models

A pertinent question is whether a specific house of prayer may combine other models. I believe the answer is "yes". As the Lord clarified our vision at Succat Hallel, we knew we were called to be a 24/7 house of prayer (we have been 24/7 for over fifteen years), as well as a city-wide, inter-congregational house of prayer, and an apostolic hub to train and send out teams to the surrounding nations.

We received and implemented our mandates and models over a period of time, as the Lord directed, and as He established Succat Hallel.

May each house of prayer know its specific calling and identity from the Lord, and may we all appreciate, acknowledge, support and love all the colors of the Body of Messiah.

CHAPTER 13

Keys to Governmental Intercession

And of the increase of His government and peace there shall be no end, upon the throne of David and over his kingdom.
—Isaiah 9:7 (KJV)

Spiritual Weapons Are Launched From the Mouth

In the battle between the Kingdom of God and the kingdom of darkness, much of the spiritual warfare over our cities and nations has to do with truth and lies; and *both* are launched through the mouth. Words make an impact, whether for good or for evil. Our enemy understands the power of the airwaves, and thus is continually spewing lies. We see this illustrated in Revelation 16:13–14:

13 Then I saw three impure spirits that looked like frogs; they came out of the mouth of the dragon, out of the mouth of the beast and out of the mouth of the false prophet. 14 They are demonic spirits that perform signs, and they go out to the kings of the whole world, to gather them for the battle on the great day of God Almighty.

We have experienced this in a very real way in Jerusalem during our nineteen years of living here. Within hearing distance of our home, five mosques broadcast their "call to prayer" from minarets. Each time we notice a change in the tone of the call to prayer to something more aggressive-sounding, usually accompanied by increased volume, acts of radical Islamic violence follow soon afterwards. Other believers who live in our area have observed the same.

We need to realize the power of the audible proclamation of truth, whether spoken or sung. Sometimes we battle this way during "high praise". There are times in a prophetic flow that the Holy Spirit leads us into strong, almost militant praise. This is scriptural, and was clearly the norm in the Tabernacle of David, as evidenced in Psalm 149:5–9:

5 Let the godly ones exult in glory;

Let them sing for joy on their beds.

*6 Let the high praises of God be in their **mouths**,*

And a two-edged sword in their hand,

7 To execute vengeance on the nations

And punishment on the peoples,

8 To bind their kings with chains

And their nobles with fetters of iron,

9 To execute on them the judgment written;

This is an honor for all His godly ones.

Praise the Lord! (NASB; emphasis added).

As the *"high praises"* are in our mouths, and the *"two-edged sword"* (the scriptures; see Hebrews 4:12) is in our hands, we administer or execute His judgments on the nations and their governmental leaders, both natural and spiritual (verses 7–9). We can only carry out those judgments that He has already declared, but our administration of them is effective in changing the nations, and is an honor for us!

Why is it so important that truth needs to be not just in our hearts

> **The very atmosphere over our cities and nations responds to what is proclaimed aloud by mouth (Proverbs 11:11).**

or minds, but also launched from our mouths? I (Rick) believe part of the answer is that Satan and demonic powers are *not* omniscient, and they cannot read our thoughts as God does. They respond according to what they hear.

Thus, in some way, the very atmosphere over our cities and nations responds to what is proclaimed aloud by mouth: *"By the blessing of the upright a city is exalted, but **by the mouth** of the wicked it is torn down"* (Proverbs 11:11, NASB; emphasis added). Even children can help change the atmosphere over a city, as they declare from their mouths the praises of God: *"Through the praise of children and infants you have established a stronghold against your enemies, **to silence** the foe and the avenger"* (Psalm 8:2; emphasis added).

Notice that the vocal praises of those in the Kingdom of God actually help silence the vocal launching of lies by the demonic realm. I believe that in this spiritual battle of truth versus lies, it is almost as if the enemy is only launching low-tech "Scud" missiles. If not counteracted, they can still do a lot of damage.

But when we speak out truth from our mouths, with the high praises of God in our mouths, we are launching the "high-tech" missiles of the Lord. Much like the Iron Dome missiles invented by Israel, these verbal missiles can actually go into the heavenlies and destroy the low-tech missiles fired by the enemy!

2 Corinthians 10:3–5 declares:

3 For though we live in the world, we do not wage war as the world does. 4 The weapons we fight with are not the weapons of the world. On the contrary, they have divine power to demolish strongholds. 5 We demolish arguments and every pretension that sets itself up against the knowledge of God, and we take captive every thought to make it obedient to Christ.

Confessing a City or Nation's Sin Is Foundational

The prophet Daniel is perhaps the best example of a governmental intercessor in the Bible. Even after many years of exile, he still carried the burden for his native Jerusalem in his heart. He knew the atmosphere could only be changed over Jerusalem if there was an identificational confession of the sins of the city of his forefathers. As he fasted, here is what he prayed for that specific geographical location, in Daniel 9:4–9; 17–19:

> 4 I prayed to the Lord my God and confessed: "Lord, the great and awesome God, who keeps His covenant of love with those who love Him and keep His commandments, 5 we have sinned and done wrong. We have been wicked and have rebelled; we have turned away from Your commands and laws. 6 We have not listened to Your servants the prophets, who spoke in Your name to our kings, our princes and our ancestors, and to all the people of the land.

> 7 "Lord, You are righteous, but this day we are covered with shame—the people of Judah and the inhabitants of Jerusalem and all Israel, both near and far, in all the countries where You have scattered us because of our unfaithfulness to You. 8 We and our kings, our princes and our ancestors are covered with shame, Lord, because we have sinned against You. 9 The Lord our God is merciful and forgiving, even though we have rebelled against Him …. 17 Now, our God, hear the prayers and petitions of Your servant. For Your sake, Lord, look with favor on Your desolate sanctuary. 18 Give ear, our God, and hear; open Your eyes and see the desolation of the city that bears Your Name. We do not make requests of You because we are righteous, but because of Your great mercy. 19 Lord, listen! Lord, forgive! Lord, hear and act! For Your sake, my God, do not delay, because Your city and Your people bear Your Name."

Notice that Daniel did not pray for his city or nation in a proud, critical way, saying, "*They* have sinned." Instead, he identified with the sins of his forefathers, city, and nation, praying, "*We* have sinned." And his prayers helped release the return of the Israelite exiles, and the restoration of Jerusalem.

In chapter 3, "Preparing a Dwelling Place for the Lord," I testified of several years of such prayer in the Ben Hinnom Valley in Jerusalem, resulting—by God's grace—with a spiritual and very visible physical transformation of the valley.

Another testimony of the power of prayers for the identificational confession of sin took place in the nation of Zambia, when the corporate confession of national sin helped stop a locust plague.

In 1996 I (Rick) had the privilege of speaking at a prayer conference in Zambia, a poor nation in central Africa. The host pastor explained that their biggest challenge at that time was a locust plague that was headed toward Zambia. He said a previous plague had led to large numbers of deaths from starvation.

I then said, "Let's start at the throne of the Lord in worship, and then see how He directs us to pray."

After a time of powerful worship, the anointing of the Holy Spirit was released in the room, and the Zambian pastors and intercessors started confessing the sins of their nation. They did so, identifying with the people like the prophet Daniel did, and weeping for their nation and its sins.

When that sovereign time of confession of sin ended, I sensed the Holy Spirit say that we were "authorized" to command the locust plague not to enter Zambia.

I shared with my African pastor friend who was leading the conference what I was sensing. He agreed. So we asked everyone to stand up and repeat phrase by phrase something like this: "In the Name and by the blood of Jesus Christ, we say to you, locust plague, that you will stop at the borders of this country, and you will *not* enter Zambia."

Soon after I got home, the pastor sent me a fax showing this headline from the 22 May 1996 edition of *The Times of Zambia*: "Locust Plagues Miraculously Evade Zambia." He said that on television, a United Nations expert even called it a "miracle", saying that in his many years of study, he had never heard of a locust plague getting right to the border, and then turning and going in another direction!

Unity and Spiritual Protection Are Essential

In chapter 14, "The Crown and Throne Paradigm," I will describe in greater detail how we proclaimed a spiritual earthquake to expose corruption in Israel's government. Before proclaiming such a radical thing, I first ran it by the leader of that watch, Guy Kump, to confirm this was not just my political opinion, which was a safeguard for me. We saw the result with a physical earthquake twenty minutes later, and eventually the rest of the prophecy came to pass.

Many people who feel drawn to governmental prayer have been disappointed because they believed so fervently in the political opinion they'd been praying. But they had not heard from God. The Lord has sometimes stopped me from praying my opinion out loud, helping me to realize I had not really heard from Him. God is like a master chess player who is always several moves ahead of his opponent in his thoughts, and will sometimes lose one position on the chess board in order to win the final game.

How then do we keep from praying our political opinion, thinking we have somehow heard the Lord? How do we avoid doing or saying things that are soulish, foolish, or even spiritually dangerous?

I believe the key lies in mutual submission with other spiritually mature intercessors. When the warfare moves to larger issues over a city or nation, there is great protection in the counsel of mature intercessors, host peoples (the native peoples of that region), and pastors or ministry leaders who are recognized as spiritual elders in that city, region, or nation. Proverbs 24:6 states: *"Surely you need guidance to wage war, and victory is won through many advisers."*

Part of the restoration of the Tabernacle of David is the restoration of godly order in intercessory and worship ministries. In 1 Chronicles 25:1–3, it is written that David worked together with his military commanders to appoint chief musicians Asaph, Heman, and Jeduthun for the ministry of prophesying accompanied by their musical instruments. In turn, the sons of each of these three worship leaders prophesied under the supervision of their fathers.

There is much spiritual protection and wisdom when we learn to flow in this ministry in an intergenerational way, and are under godly spiritual authority (not oppression or control, but humble spiritual fatherhood and motherhood).

In our governmental intercession watches at Succat Hallel, we ask someone to serve as the prayer leader and monitor. That way, people clear with them the basic idea of what they will pray before they take the microphone. This is especially important, because we have many visitors from various nations each week, many of them wonderful intercessors, but unknown to us.

This principle is in line with the role of elders or rulers at the gates of cities or nations, which is discussed in more depth in chapter 14, "The Crown and Throne Paradigm." It is illustrated in the example below.

Elders at the City Gates Close Demonic Doors

In 2006, a worldwide, weeklong gay pride event was planned for Jerusalem that intended to bring over one hundred thousand homosexuals to the city for a week of partying. This had only happened previously in one other city, Rome. Although we love the sinners, we do not want to love the sin, and did not want to see doors opened for greater demonic activity in the city. A group of pastors and ministry leaders began to meet one morning each week to pray about this event.

A group of Orthodox Jewish rabbis in Jerusalem asked the Supreme Court for an injunction against this event as not being in the character of what is called "the holy city". We prayed for the Supreme Court to be favorable to their petition, but the Court said that Israel was to be a modern, pluralistic society like Western nations, and had to allow such an event to take place.

About two weeks before the event was scheduled to take place, we were praying about what to do. By now, most hotels in the city had been fully booked for this event.

As we were praying, I sensed the Lord saying, "There is a time to ask and there is a time to command. This is a time to command as 'elders in the gates of the city' that the doors be closed to this event." I shared this with the other pastors and leaders. They agreed. We stood together, looking out a window over the city, and proclaimed: "In the Name and by the blood of *Yeshua*, we proclaim that the gates of Jerusalem are closed to this event!"

About two weeks later, just a few days before the event was to start, an Islamic terrorist group, Hezbollah, started firing many missiles from southern Lebanon into northern Israel. Even though the missiles did not do great damage, they were numerous. The Israeli army announced on the media something like this: "Because we need so many of our troops on the northern border and need to be prepared for war, we cannot provide security for civilian events. Therefore, *all* civilian events of over one thousand people are cancelled until further notice."

In a creative way that we would never have thought of, the Lord backed up our proclamation of His decree that the gates of Jerusalem were to be closed to this event. The organizers were very angry because they lost huge sums of money, and they posted on their website: "We will never again plan an event in Jerusalem."

We said, "Amen."

CHAPTER 14

The Crown and Throne Paradigm

And [He] has made us kings and priest to His God and Father,
to Him be glory and dominion forever and ever.

—Revelation 1:6 (NKJV)

An Earthquake Shook Our Nation After Prayer

On 11 February 2008, several of us gathered at a weekly watch at Succat Hallel where we prayed for the government of our nation. As we were worshipping and praying, I sensed the Holy Spirit said we were to proclaim "an earthquake into the foundations of the government of Israel to expose corruption in all political parties, and to uproot Prime Minister [Ehud] Olmert from office." I was taken by surprise at the audacity of what I felt we were to proclaim. I shared what I sensed with Guy Kump, one of our leaders who oversaw that watch. Guy has an anointing in governmental intercession and had served as executive director of Intercessors for America for nine years before he moved to Israel. Guy confirmed what I sensed we should proclaim, which helped me to know that this was not just my personal political opinion.

So we proclaimed with one voice: "Let there be an earthquake into the foundations of the government of Israel to expose corruption in all political parties, and let Prime Minister Olmert be removed from office."

About twenty minutes later, Jerusalem was rocked by a literal, physical earthquake that measured 5.3 on the Richter scale!

Amazingly enough, the exposure of one corruption scandal after another unfolded over the next few months. Finally, Prime Minister Olmert was forced to tender his resignation on 30 July 2008.

After a long legal process, on 31 March 2014, the former prime minister was convicted of corruption and bribery (and later sentenced to prison). *The Jerusalem Post* published a report with the headline: "Thundering Ruling Shakes Country." How amazed we were that they used the word "shakes" to describe what we had been told to proclaim as an "earthquake" into the political realm in 2008!

Former Prime Minister Olmert was not the only one convicted by the judge. *The Jerusalem Post* reported:

> Completing nearly two years of what may be looked back on as the trial of the century, the Tel Aviv District Court ... convicted former prime minister Ehud Olmert on charges of bribery.
>
> With a thundering ruling that will shake the country, Judge David Rozen also convicted former Jerusalem Mayor Uri Lupolianski, former Bank Hapoalim Chairman Dan Dankner, Olmert's former chief-of-staff Shula Zaken and, in total, 10 out of 13 individual defendants (3 defendants are corporations.)

I am not talking here about praying our political opinions. I've tried that before, and was disappointed. The scriptures make clear in Lamentations 3:37: *"Who can speak and have it happen if the Lord has not decreed it?"* What I just described is a good example of the governmental intercession and worship that I would term "crown and throne intercession and worship".

The Crown and Throne Paradigm

The past twenty years have been a time of the revelation of "harp and bowl," the joy of joining the power of worship and prayer together. In Revelation 5:8, *"the twenty-four elders fell down before the Lamb. Each one had a harp and they were holding golden bowls full of incense, which are the prayers of God's people."*

Yet a "harp and bowl" are not the only items the elders in the book of Revelation had. They also each had a "crown and throne." I believe the next twenty years (should the Lord tarry) will be a time of greatly increased revelation of the "crown and throne." Revelation 4:2–4 states:

> *2 At once I was in the Spirit, and there before me was a throne in heaven with Someone sitting on it. 3 And the one who sat there had the appearance of jasper and ruby. A rainbow that shone like an emerald encircled the throne. 4 Surrounding the throne were twenty-four other thrones, and seated on them were twenty-four elders. They were dressed in white and had crowns of gold on their heads.*

> I believe the next twenty years (should the Lord tarry) will be a time of greatly increased revelation of the "crown and throne."

The past twenty years in the house of prayer movement have been a time of rediscovering our role as *priests* ministering to the Lord. We have been rediscovering the joy of intimacy with the Lord, and of priestly intercession on behalf of people, cities, and nations.

Prayer Movements in Transition

I believe a great focus of the Holy Spirit in this next season is to rediscover our role as *kings*—those who sit in the gates of cities and nations to execute and administer the decrees of the *King of Kings*. As priests, we are called to ministry *to* the Lord. As kings, we are called to ministry *from* the Lord. To see the fullness of the restoration of the Tabernacle of David, we need to see both the priestly and the kingly anointings expressed in the house of prayer. My friend Don Crum first shared with me the term "crown and throne" to describe the governmental intercession and worship that we both had been operating in.

When I shared this with another friend, Jon Hamill, he shared with me a vision he had had of three jets that he felt represented three different "streams". In the prayer movement: the strategic-prayer stream *takes* territory; the house of prayer/ministry to the Lord stream *possesses or occupies* that territory; and the "crown and throne" prayer/governmental-intercession stream executes the Kingdom of God's *rule* over that territory. I believe that all three kinds of prayer are needed to see the enemy's thrones crumble, and the Lord's throne established over specific geographical locations. We must learn to respect and see the need for each other's emphases and strengths to see the government of God increase where He has positioned us.

Governmental Rooting and Uprooting

The prophet Jeremiah was called to prophetic governmental intercession in the womb, and installed into his calling as a youth! His calling is described in Jeremiah 1:4–10:

> 4 *The word of the Lord came to me, saying, 5 "Before I formed you in the womb I knew you, before you were born I set you apart; I appointed you as a prophet to the nations." 6 "Alas, Sovereign Lord," I said, "I do not know how to speak; I am too young." 7 But the Lord said to me, "Do not say, 'I am too young.' You must go to everyone I send you to and say whatever I command you. 8 Do not be afraid of them, for I am with you and will rescue you," declares the Lord. 9 Then the Lord reached out His hand and touched my mouth and said to me, "**I have put My words in your mouth. 10 See, today I appoint you over nations and kingdoms to uproot and tear down, to destroy and overthrow, to build and to plant.**"* (emphasis added)

As the Lord raises up a company of prophetic intercessors in our day, it's important to realize that:

(1) Certain intercessors are called to this specific kind of prayer.

(2) They will experience the Lord "putting His words in their mouths." The words they're given to proclaim may have both positive and negative effects (uproot, plant, etc.)

(3) When they proclaim what He has given them, it will have a measurable impact, even on nations.

Kings and Priests

For "crown and throne" intercession to become a normal, functioning part of our houses of prayer, we need a paradigm shift. Like Queen Esther, we are invited to come into the revelation of our true "royal" identity, so we may have the boldness to step out in this kind of prayer.

We need to realize that we are called not only as communities or congregations, but that we also have a "congressional" or ecclesiastical calling to execute His decrees over specific geographical areas.

> For "crown and throne" intercession to become a normal, functioning part of our houses of prayer, we need a paradigm shift.

In ancient times, the elders of a city sat at the city gates and heard cases to determine whether or not something or someone would be allowed in. This is seen clearly in Joshua 20:4: *"When they flee to one of these cities, they are to stand in the entrance of the city gate and state their case before the elders of that city. Then the elders are to admit the fugitive into their city and provide a place to live among them."*

Jesus (Yeshua) refers to this concept in Matthew 16:18–19:

> *18 I say to you that you are Peter, and upon this rock I will build My church; and the gates of Hades will not overpower it. 19 I will give you the keys of the kingdom of heaven; and whatever you bind on earth shall have been bound in heaven,*

and whatever you loose on earth shall have been loosed in heaven. (NASB)

The word Yeshua uses in this passage for "church" is the Greek word *ecclesia*. We tend to think of "church" only in terms of an assembly of believers, a congregation. It is that, but it is also more. The word *ecclesia* was also consistently used of a group of elders in a city called together as a legislative body to make important decisions and decrees on behalf of the city.

Jesus is not describing a tame congregation whose members enjoy their community while the enemy invades their city. He is talking about a legislative body arising that can make a difference in the future of their city or nation.

When He speaks of the "gates of Hades" (hell), He is using military terminology. We actually are to go on the military offensive to the point where we reach the gates of the enemy and thwart His plans. The word here for "gates" is not the one used for small gates, like the gate of a house, but for the massive, strong gates that protect ancient fortresses and cities.

This promise was first given to the seed of Abraham in Genesis 22:17: *"Blessing I will bless you, and multiplying I will multiply your descendants as the stars of the heaven and as the sand which is on the seashore; and your descendants shall possess the gate of their enemies"* (NKJV).

Since we are grafted into the Hebrew people of God (see Romans 11:17, 24), and are spiritual "descendants" of Abraham, we also have a calling to possess the gates of our enemies.

But what does it mean that we are to "possess" the gates of our enemies, and how does this enable us to possess the gates of our cities and nations? The Hebrew word translated "possess" here can mean: "to occupy by driving out previous tenants, then possessing in their place. To seize, to inherit, to expel, to impoverish (starve an enemy out by cutting off his supply line), to ruin, dispossess."[4]

---

4   James Strong, *Strong's Exhaustive Concordance of the Bible* (Nashville, TN: Thomas Nelson, 1992.

How do we go about doing that?

Proclamation Prayer Administers His Will

To make the powerful arsenal that God has supplied to us fully operational, we need to grasp more fully that "proclamation prayers," as revealed and grounded in the scriptures, are very much tied to executing the Lord's will for the specific geographical locations over which He has given us mandates.

This becomes clearer when we understand how ancient systems of law and their enforcement worked in a kingdom. When a king decreed a new law for his kingdom, it was not enforced in a specific city until a herald sent by the king arrived in that city, sounded the trumpet to gather the people, and proclaimed aloud the king's decree. This pattern is clear in Daniel 3:4–11:

> 4 Then **the herald loudly proclaimed**, 'Nations and peoples of every language, this is what you are commanded to do: 5 As soon as you hear the sound of the horn, flute, zither, lyre, harp, pipe and all kinds of music, you must fall down and worship the image of gold that King Nebuchadnezzar has set up. 6 Whoever does not fall down and worship will immediately be thrown into a blazing furnace.'
>
> 7 Therefore, as soon as they heard the sound of the horn, flute, zither, lyre, harp and all kinds of music, all the nations and peoples of every language fell down and worshiped the image of gold that King Nebuchadnezzar had set up. 8 At this time some astrologers came forward and denounced the Jews. 9 They said to King Nebuchadnezzar, 'May the king live forever! 10 **Your Majesty has issued a decree** that everyone who hears the sound of the horn, flute, zither, lyre, harp, pipe and all kinds of music must fall down and worship the image of gold, 11 and that whoever does not fall down and worship will be thrown into a blazing furnace.' (emphasis added)

I (Rick) was further encouraged that Holy Spirit-led proclamation prayer is scriptural as I realized that the prophet Jeremiah sent Seraiah (his servant Baruch's brother) to Babylon to proclaim a prophecy the Lord had given to Jeremiah:

> 59 This is the message Jeremiah the prophet gave to the staff officer Seraiah ... when he went to Babylon with Zedekiah king of Judah .... 60 Jeremiah had written on a scroll about all the disasters that would come upon Babylon—all that had been recorded concerning Babylon. 61 He said to Seraiah, "When you get to Babylon, see that you read all these words aloud. 62 Then say, 'Lord, You have said You will destroy this place, so that neither people nor animals will live in it; it will be desolate forever.' 63 When you finish reading this scroll, tie a stone to it and throw it into the Euphrates. 64 Then say, 'So will Babylon sink to rise no more because of the disaster I will bring on her. And her people will fall.'" (Jeremiah 51:59–64)

In a modern-day example, a proclamation made in Jerusalem on 11 February 2004 had a measurable effect. We had been in a season of much prayer and proclamation concerning the Temple Mount in Jerusalem. As we worshipped, I suddenly felt an urgency from the Holy Spirit to immediately proclaim aloud Psalm 99. It begins with these words: "The Lord reigns, let the nations tremble; He sits enthroned between the cherubim, let the earth shake." The psalm ends in verse 9 with a reference to the Temple Mount: "Exalt the Lord our God and worship at His holy mountain, for the Lord our God is holy."

The very moment I declared "holy"—the last word of the psalm—the light fixtures started to swing, and the room began to sway, as an earthquake measuring over 5.0 on the Richter scale hit Jerusalem! So the earth did shake, just as I had proclaimed from verse 1!

When the earthquake subsided, one of our intercessors, Una Gere, said that as I stood up to proclaim Psalm 99, she received a scripture in Revelation 11 that also speaks of an earthquake in Jerusalem.

Local papers reported that, amazingly enough, there had been little damage from the earthquake other than a big crack that appeared in the roof of the Dome of the Rock Mosque on the Temple Mount!

Possessing the Mediterranean Gate to Israel

In June 2010, a few of us met with a small group of intercessors led by Avi Mizrachi, a messianic Jewish pastor in Tel Aviv, a city on the Mediterranean coast. He and I poured salt (representing covenant) and oil (representing the work of the Holy Spirit) into the waters of the Mediterranean Sea, and we all proclaimed together, "Let life and not death come out of these waters, in the name of the Lord *Yeshua ha Mashiah*"! (Hebrew for "Jesus Christ"). This prophetic action was based on a story about the prophet Elisha in 2 Kings 2:19–22:

> *19 The people of the city said to Elisha, "Look, our lord, this town is well situated, as you can see, but the water is bad and the land is unproductive." 20 "Bring me a new bowl," he said, "and put salt in it." So they brought it to him. 21 Then he went out to the spring and threw the salt into it, saying, "This is what the Lord says: 'I have healed this water. Never again will it cause death or make the land unproductive.'" 22 And the water has remained pure to this day, according to the word Elisha had spoken.*

Those proclamations, based on prophetic revelation received in worship, proved to be very practical and timely. In January 2011, I was led to share the shark vision at Succat Hallel again, and for us to pray in a renewed way for protection from military threats from the Mediterranean. (For the full vision, see chapter 11, "A Prophetic Flow of Praise, Worship and Prayer.")

On 25 January 2011, a revolution began in Egypt, with millions taking to the streets and demanding the ouster of President Hosni Mubarak. In a YouTube prayer alert on 2 February, I stated a revelation I had received: "If Mubarak is overthrown, expect to see Iran try to bring ships through the Suez Canal and into the Mediterranean." I shared this with a man high in security, who took it seriously. A different believer at the U.S. Pentagon who heard what I had said told me that would be "impossible." But on 11 February, Mubarak resigned as president of Egypt, and on 22 February, two Iranian ships sailed through the Suez Canal and into the Mediterranean!

I do not know if it was because of the prophetic revelation I had shared with the man high in security circles, but Israeli intelligence carefully tracked the two Iranian ships. The ships offloaded their "cargo" in Syria to another ship. That ship headed toward the Gaza/Egyptian shoreline, where it was boarded by Israeli officials for inspection. The captain claimed he was only transporting "cotton and lentils." *The Israeli officials insisted on inspecting, and found under the "cotton and lentils" over fifty tons of weapons and six missiles, each capable of sinking a ship!*

We believe many lives were protected by what came out of revelation received during prophetic worship.

In July 2011, we took about fifty of our staff and their families on a boat along the border in the Mediterranean Sea between Israel and Lebanon. We were led to pour salt into the water and proclaim once again: "Let life and not death come out of these waters, in the Name of the Lord *Yeshua ha Mashiah.*"

Not only was death stopped from coming out of the waters of the Mediterranean, but something life-giving came out of those same waters. In December 2010 and June 2012, huge gas fields were discovered in the territorial waters of Israel. Before that discovery, Israel had been dependent for much of its natural gas on Egypt, and the pipelines were often sabotaged by Islamic militant groups. With these gas discoveries, Israel will no longer be dependent on Egypt for gas, but Israel will become one of the greatest exporters of natural gas to Europe. Life came out of the waters instead of death!

Prophetic Revelation Helped Set Back Iran's Nuclear Program

On 8 November 2011, during strong prophetic worship at Succat Hallel, I (Rick) received a vision concerning Iran: I saw waves of cleansing going out from the Middle Eastern houses of prayer to prepare the way across the Middle East.

I then saw a Tower of Babel being built in Iran, representing a working together of various nations to stand against God. I sensed it represented their nuclear weapons programs. As they were bringing the final stones to place them on top, lightning from heaven struck it, and the top level of stones fell off, producing a setback to their nuclear efforts.

Then waves of water coming from the worship of the houses of prayer in the Middle East washed away sand in Iran, and uncovered and exposed hidden things.

In that same time period, my wife Patricia received a dream in the night in which she entered an elevator with two scientists and descended deep into a mountain, where she then saw a very specific type of blue tiles. Later in the dream, the elevator could no longer be used to get back up out of the mountain. When she later felt to "google" Iranian tiles, she saw the exact same type of blue tiles that she had seen in her dream.

Just four days after I received the vision of a setback to the Iranian nuclear program, a report on a military intelligence website (Debka. com, 12 November 2011), published this headline: "Iran loses its top missile expert in explosions sparked by failed bid to fit nuclear warhead on Shahab-3." The report said that the explosion took place forty-six kilometers west of Tehran, and was strong enough to "shatter windows and damage shops in Tehran." A highly placed security official I know, who did not want his name revealed, confirmed the report was true.

A little over a year later, another big explosion shook Iran's Fordow nuclear development facility. As reported by World Net Daily on 24 January 2013: "According to a source in the security forces protecting Fordow, *an explosion on Monday at 11:30 a.m. Tehran time rocked the site, which is buried deep under a mountain and immune not only to airstrikes but to most bunker-buster bombs*," reported Hamidreza Zakeri, formerly with the Islamic regime's Ministry of Intelligence and National Security (emphasis added).

By two days later in the afternoon, rescue workers had still failed to reach the trapped personnel. *The site, about three-hundred feet under a mountain, had two elevators, which at the time of writing were out of commission.* One elevator descended about 240 feet to reach centrifuge chambers. The other went to the bottom to carry heavy equipment and transfer uranium hexafluoride. One emergency staircase reaches the bottom of the site and another one was not complete. The source said the emergency exit southwest of the site was "unreachable."[5]

This is quite remarkable, given that in Patricia's dream, the exit out of the mountain tunnel was blocked.

Praise God that we can say with the prophet Daniel:

> 20 Praise be to the name of God for ever and ever;
>
> wisdom and power are His.
>
> 21 He changes times and seasons;
>
> He deposes kings and raises up others.
>
> He gives wisdom to the wise
>
> and knowledge to the discerning.
>
> 22 He reveals deep and hidden things;
>
> He knows what lies in darkness,
>
> and light dwells with Him." (Daniel 2:20–22)

Discern the Right Moment for Proclamation Prayer

In the testimony of the locust plague stopped from entering Zambia (see Chapter 13, "Keys to Governmental Intercession"), you may have noticed that it was only after the corporate confession of national sins that I sensed we'd been "authorized" to command the locust plague to not cross the border. I see a difference between "authority" and "authorization". As believers, we have "authority" in the name and by the blood of the Lord Jesus Christ (*Yeshua ha Mashiah*) over demonic and natural situations; but "authorization" comes when the Commander of the armies of heaven says, "Shoot now!" A good soldier waits for the "authorization" of his commanding officer.

Even as we grow in discerning when the Lord really has put His words in our mouths, we also grow in hearing when to release the power of His words through our mouths.

---

5   www.wnd.com/2013/01/sabotage-key-iranian-nuclear-facility-hit/#qvyj8duvrCPgV1OF.03

In Jeremiah 1:9–10 above, the Lord spoke of the power of releasing the words He would put in the prophet's mouth concerning the nations. But Jeremiah waited until the Lord said it was time to proclaim those words: *"The word of the Lord came to me: 'Go and proclaim in the hearing of Jerusalem…"* (Jeremiah 2:1–2).

Keep Proclamation in Perspective

Proclamation prayer does not produce measurable results just because it's declared out loud. Like Jeremiah in chapter 1:4–10, we need the Lord to put *His* words in our mouths. Lamentations 3:37 explains: *"Who can speak and have it happen if the Lord has not decreed it?"* That is why confirmation from other recognized, mature intercessors is so important.

Of course, we will not see every situation change and the fullness of the Kingdom of God on earth until Yeshua returns. We can only open doors on earth that He has declared open from heaven, and we can only close doors on earth that He has declared closed in heaven. May the Lord give us all grace to wait on Him for His clear direction, to see that confirmed by other mature intercessors, and then to release city- or nation-changing proclamations.

> Proclamation prayer does not produce measurable results just because it's declared out loud. We need the Lord to put His words in our mouths.

CHAPTER 15

Standing With Israel

Foreigners will rebuild your walls, and their kings will serve you.
Though in anger I struck you, in favor I will show you compassion.
—Isaiah 60:10

I (Rick) did not come to a revelation of God's heart for Israel because I was in a family or church with that revelation. Although my family was not against Israel, three generations had lived and ministered for parts of their lives in Egypt. So it was more natural for me to have a focus on Egypt.

However, as I sought the Lord, desiring to know Him more and to know His heart more deeply, I began to realize there were many scriptures underlining His deep heart love for Israel and the Jewish people. I also realized that this truth did not in any way diminish His infinite love for other peoples as well, including all those of the Middle East.

But I began to understand that Israel has unique covenants, and a unique calling among the nations in its role as His "firstborn son." In Exodus 4:22–23, the Lord reveals His heart as He tells Moses: *"Say to Pharaoh, 'This is what the Lord says: Israel is My firstborn son, and I told you, "Let My son go, so he may worship Me. But you refused to let him go; so I will kill your firstborn son.'"* Obviously, there are serious consequences if one seeks to interfere with God's plans for His "firstborn son".

> **If we desire to know the heart of the Lord more deeply, we have an Israel mandate: to pray for Israel to fulfill its calling as His firstborn son.**

What does it mean to be a firstborn son? As of this writing, we have fourteen grandchildren. Our eldest daughter has eight children. Their firstborn is named Josiah, and his Hebrew nickname is "Yoshi". I sometimes hear Yoshi's mother or father reminding him that he is the "firstborn son"—and that therefore, he has a unique role to play: to set a good example spiritually and behaviorally for the others to follow. I sometimes hear his mother or father asking him to help get the younger children ready to go, etc. But occasionally, the younger children complain because Yoshi gets to stay up later at night. In other words, a firstborn has unique responsibilities and privileges.

If we desire to know the heart of the Lord more deeply, we have an Israel mandate: to pray for Israel to fulfill its calling as His firstborn son. But we also have an Israel mandate because we are called to *"prepare the way of the Lord"* in these end times (see Isaiah 40:1–3), in which Israel is called to play a central role.

Israel and God's Prophetic Timeline

Israel's restoration is linked to the restored Tabernacle of David and the end-time harvest. I believe these three, great, end-time purposes of God are intertwined, as revealed in Amos 9:11–15:

> 11 *"On that day I will raise up*
>
> *The tabernacle of David, which has fallen down,*
>
> *And repair its damages;*
>
> *I will raise up its ruins,*
>
> *And rebuild it as in the days of old;*
>
> 12 *That they may possess the remnant of Edom,*

And all the Gentiles who are called by My name,"

Says the Lord who does this thing.

13 'Behold, the days are coming," says the Lord,

"When the plowman shall overtake the reaper,

And the treader of grapes him who sows seed;

The mountains shall drip with sweet wine,

And all the hills shall flow with it.

14 I will bring back the captives of My people Israel;

They shall build the waste cities and inhabit them;

They shall plant vineyards and drink wine from them;

They shall also make gardens and eat fruit from them.

15 I will plant them in their land,

And no longer shall they be pulled up

From the land I have given them,"

Says the Lord your God. (NKJV)

Restoration of the Tabernacle of David

In verses 11–12 above, Amos prophesies the restoration of *"the tabernacle of David, which has fallen down."* We believe this prophetic word is foundational to our understanding and practice in the house of prayer, and that the current worldwide multiplication of houses of prayer in part fulfills the Lord's promise to restore the fallen Tabernacle of David.

Briefly, when David wanted to bring back the ark of the covenant (the place of God's manifested Presence) that had been lost to the Philistines because of Israel's idolatry and rebellion, the Lord did not tell him to put it back in the old Tabernacle of Moses. God did not instruct him to place it in the rather isolated location where it had been

> The future throne of David, on which Jesus (Yeshua) will sit, will be established the same way as the original throne of David–through 24/7 worship and prayer.

before, but instead to erect a new tent for it in the middle of his new capital city, Jerusalem.

I believe Amos's prophecy of the restoration of the Tabernacle of David refers not only to the restoration of the fallen house or throne of David, upon which Yeshua must sit to reign. It also implies that the future throne of David, on which Jesus (Yeshua) will sit, will be established the same way as the original throne of David—through 24/7 worship and prayer.

Amos says part of the purpose of the restoration of the Tabernacle of David is *"that they may possess the remnant of Edom, and all the Gentiles who are called by My name"* (Amos 9:12).

This seems to indicate that the restoration of the Tabernacle of David will bring the Kingdom of the Son of David to bear upon Edom—the descendants of Esau in the Middle East. It could also potentially refer to a great harvest among Middle Eastern Muslims (who identify with Esau). They are very impressed when they find out that we do not pray and worship only five times a day, as Muslims do, but 24/7!

Restoration of the Accelerated Harvest

But Amos goes even further to say that this restoration will affect all *"the Gentiles who are called by My name"* (verse 12). This brings us to the second great end-time purpose of God prophesied by Amos: the restoration of the accelerated harvest.

"Behold, the days are coming," says the Lord,
"When the plowman shall overtake the reaper,
And the treader of grapes him who sows seed;
The mountains shall drip with sweet wine,
And all the hills shall flow with it." (Amos 9:13)

Though there have been a few seasons of accelerated harvest since the first one on the day of Pentecost (*Shavuot*) and the weeks following (see Acts 2), they have been few and far between. But in our days, as the worship and prayer movement explodes worldwide, we are seeing millions quickly being swept into the Kingdom of God in places such as the Far East, parts of Africa, and Central and South America.

I believe Amos not only is prophesying of the restoration of a literal harvest of crops in Israel, but he also is prophesying of a future, accelerated spiritual harvest in the nations. This work has already begun. (For examples of accelerated harvest in Algeria and Indonesia, please see chapter 19, "Watching Over the Harvest.")

Restoration of Israel

The theme of restoration continues as Amos prophesies over Israel:

14 "I will bring back the captives of My people Israel;
They shall build the waste cities and inhabit them;
They shall plant vineyards and drink wine from them;
They shall also make gardens and eat fruit from them.
15 I will plant them in their land,
And no longer shall they be pulled up
From the land I have given them,"
says the Lord your God. (Amos 9:14–15 NKJV)

I believe this third element of the Amos 9 prophecy gives us a timetable as to when to expect the restoration of both the Tabernacle of David and the accelerated harvest. They are to take place when the Lord restores the exiled Jewish people back to their Land, never again to be uprooted. I have ministered many times in about fifty nations; and often, in countries such as China and Indonesia, many cities already are experiencing the multiplication of houses of prayer and the accelerated harvest. It is interesting to me that in most of these places, there is also a profound revelation of the heart of God for the physical and spiritual restoration of Israel.

I believe what happens in Israel has a spiritual ripple effect in the nations. It is no coincidence that in 1948, when Israel was restored as a modern state, many ministries were released that have impacted the world greatly in areas such as evangelism (Billy Graham and Bill Bright) and healing (Gordon Lindsay and Oral Roberts).

Gordon Lindsay's granddaughter shared with me that her grandfather had often said to her grandmother, "When Israel is restored as a nation, then there will be a great outpouring of healing."

The day he heard the news of Israel's independence, he ran to his wife Freda and said, "Now I can start ministering in healing, and the signs and wonders will happen." That is exactly what happened! And he also went on to found Christ for the Nations Bible Institute, which has an emphasis on prayer, worship, healing, missions, and Israel to this day.

Many have asked me, "If this is the fulfillment of prophecy, then why is there so much sin in the Holy Land"? But that is exactly what the prophet Ezekiel was shown. He describes his vision of the Jewish people coming up out of their graves, and returning to Israel as dead, dry bones: 1 *"The hand of the Lord was on me, and He brought me out by the Spirit of the Lord and set me in the middle of a valley; it was full of bones. 2 He led me back and forth among them, and I saw a great many bones on the floor of the valley,* **bones that were very dry***"* (Ezekiel 37:1–2; emphasis added).

The Lord then explains the meaning of the dry bones:

> *11 Then He said to me: 'Son of man,* **these bones are the people of Israel. They say, 'Our bones are dried up and our hope is gone; we are cut off***.' 12 Therefore prophesy and say to them: 'This is what the Sovereign Lord says:* **My people, I am going to open your graves and bring you up from them; I will bring you back to the land of Israel***. 13 Then you, My people, will know that I am the Lord, when I open your graves and bring you up from them. 14 I will put My Spirit in you and you will live, and I will settle you in your own land. Then you will know that I the Lord have spoken, and I have done it, declares the Lord.'* (Ezekiel 37:11–14; emphasis added)

In Ezekiel's vision, once the bones were back in the Land, they began to connect with one another. This is being fulfilled physically in Israel today, as Jewish people intermarry and connect relationally with Jews who had been exiled to other nations far away. French Jews are connecting with Ethiopian Jews; Iraqi and Iranian Jews are connecting with Polish and Russian Jews; Turkish Jews are connecting with American Jews, etc. *"So I prophesied as I was commanded. And as I was prophesying, there was a noise, a rattling sound, and the bones came together, bone to bone"* (Ezekiel 37:7).

But Ezekiel's vision does not stop with the spiritually dead, dry bones being connected to each other back in the Land. He is told to prophesy to the breath (Spirit) to come from the four winds to breathe upon these bones.

I believe this represents the prayer movement in the nations who are praying for the spiritual restoration of Israel, releasing the breath of the Holy Spirit from the east, west, north, and south. Finally, Ezekiel sees the spiritual restoration of Israel as the bones take on flesh and sinews, and stand on their feet as "a vast army" with the breath of God in them:

> *9 Then He said to me, "Prophesy to the breath; prophesy, son of man, and say to it, 'This is what the Sovereign Lord says:'* **"Come, breath, from the four winds and breathe into these slain, that they may live**.*"' 10 So I prophesied as He commanded me, and breath entered them; they came to life and stood up on their feet—a vast army."* (Ezekiel 37:9–10; emphasis added)

A Miraculous Convergence

As mentioned above, this great miracle of the physical and spiritual restoration of Israel is tied to the restoration of the Tabernacle of David and the restoration of the accelerated harvest. A miracle happened on the day of Israel's declaration as a modern, restored nation that I believe underlines this point.

All over the world, Jewish people read the same scripture passages in their synagogues every Shabbat (the Sabbath day of rest that begins Friday at sundown and ends Saturday at sundown).

The Declaration of Independence for the State of Israel was signed on Friday afternoon, 14 May 1948, just before Shabbat. After it was signed, many of the signatories would have gone to synagogue. One of our leadership team, the late Michael Cohen, suddenly thought one day, "I wonder what was read in the synagogues that day?"

He did some research on the Internet and discovered that they would have heard the reading aloud of the following verses:

> 11 **On that day I will raise up**
> **The tabernacle of David**, which has fallen down,
> And repair its damages;
> I will raise up its ruins,
> **And rebuild it as in the days of old**;
> 12 That they may possess the remnant of Edom,
> And all the Gentiles who are called by My name,'
> Says the Lord who does this thing.
> 13 "**Behold, the days are coming**" says the Lord,
> "**When the plowman shall overtake the reaper**,
> **And the treader of grapes him who sows seed**;
> The mountains shall drip with sweet wine,
> And all the hills shall flow with it.
> 14 **I will bring back the captives of My people Israel**;
> **They shall build the waste cities and inhabit them**;
> They shall plant vineyards and drink wine from them;
> They shall also make gardens and eat fruit from them.
> 15 **I will plant them in their land**,
> **And no longer shall they be pulled up**
> **From the land I have given them**,"
> **Says the Lord your God**.
> (Amos 9: 11–15, NKJV; emphasis added)

HALLELUJAH!

God's Name and Heart

As exciting as it is to see how key the restoration of Israel is to God's end-time plans and the fulfillment of prophecy, there are two far more important reasons to pray for Israel as a mandate in the house of prayer: our concern for God's Name and God's heart.

As we grow in intercession, we also should grow in our concern for the glory of God's Name. Israel is the only nation to which God has tied His very Name; one of His names is "the God of Israel". He has also tied His Name to

> As we grow in intercession, we also should grow in our concern for the glory of God's Name.

Jerusalem as the King of Jerusalem. When He fulfills the prophecies of His Word concerning Israel and Jerusalem, His Name is glorified. It was this concern for God's Name that led Daniel to pray:

> 17 Now, our God, hear the prayers and petitions of Your servant. For Your sake, Lord, look with favor on Your desolate sanctuary. 18 Give ear, our God, and hear; open Your eyes and see the desolation of the city **that bears Your Name**. We do not make requests of You because we are righteous, but because of Your great mercy. 19 Lord, listen! Lord, forgive! Lord, hear and act! **For Your sake, my God, do not delay, because Your city and Your people bear Your Name**. (Daniel 9:17–19; emphasis added)

Finally, we pray for Israel and Jerusalem in order to see the heart of God comforted concerning His Land and city. In Jeremiah 3:19–20, the Lord reveals that His concern for His Name as to Israel is not selfish, but that He loves Israel as a Father and a Husband:

> 19 "I Myself said,
> 'How gladly would I treat you like My children
> and give you a pleasant land,
> the most beautiful inheritance of any nation.'

I thought you would call Me 'Father'
and not turn away from following Me.
20 But like a woman unfaithful to her husband,
so you, Israel, have been unfaithful to me" ...
declares the Lord.

We need to ask the Lord to reveal not only His thoughts and plans towards Israel, but His very heart as a Father and a Husband to her.

A Living Example

When I was in Bible college, a close friend's wife left him. She fell totally away from the Lord, and lived with one man after another. Most people told my friend to forget her, and move on with his life. But he loved her deeply. He would come to my room and weep over her, crying out to God that she would return to the Lord and to him. I began to feel his heart and wept with him for her. What a joy when I saw his heart comforted as his former wife (she had divorced him) called him and explained in tears that she had returned to the Lord. She expressed her strong sorrow over her wrong decision. She said, "I know it is crazy to think you could ever forgive me and take me back as your wife."

He replied, "I forgave you long ago, and there is nothing I desire more than to be married to you once again." When they were remarried, I realized what a picture this was of the amazing long-suffering of our Lord over Israel as His Bride.

May He give us grace to not just pray with a mental comprehension

May He give us grace to pray with the suffering and love in His heart for backslidden Israel.

of His prophetic plans, but to also enter into the suffering and love in His heart for backslidden Israel. Then we will be living out the priority of standing with Israel in the house of prayer.

CHAPTER 16

The Isaiah 19 Highway

In that day there will be a highway from Egypt to Assyria.
The Assyrians will come into Egypt and the Egyptians into Assyria,
and the Egyptians will worship with the Assyrians. In that day
Israel will be the third party with Egypt and Assyria,
a blessing in the midst of the earth.

—Isaiah 19:23–24 (NASB)

One evening at Succat Hallel, Canon Andrew White, known as "the bishop of Baghdad" shared his heart concerning Iraq and its place in the prophetic fulfillment of Isaiah 19. He held up an old, worn Bible his father had been given, and who in turn had given it to Andrew. It had belonged to the famed British revivalist Smith Wigglesworth. He showed us how a huge number of verses were underlined because they had become revelation to Smith Wigglesworth. He then showed us Isaiah chapter 19, which had no verses underlined! Andrew asked us if we knew why. He said he felt it was because the revelation contained in this chapter was not for Smith Wigglesworth's generation, but for our generation.

Serving the Purposes of God in Our Generation

I believe what Canon White shared with us is true: revelations of certain Scriptures are reserved for the generation to be involved in their fulfillment. This is borne out by Acts 13:36: *"Now when David had served God's purpose in his own generation, he fell asleep."*

This Scripture had a great impact on my life when I was about 20 years old. The great British author, Arthur Wallis, referenced it in one of his books. Wallis stated that if you really wanted the best for your life, it was essential to discern the purpose of God in your generation, and then to give yourself fully to what God was doing in your time.

I believe the astounding prophecy of Isaiah 19:23–25 is one of the major purposes of God for our generation:

> *23 In that day there will be a highway from Egypt to Assyria. The Assyrians will come into Egypt and the Egyptians into Assyria, and the Egyptians will worship with the Assyrians. 24 In that day Israel will be the third party with Egypt and Assyria, a blessing in the midst of the earth, 25 whom the Lord of hosts has blessed, saying, 'Blessed is Egypt My people, and Assyria the work of My hands, and Israel My inheritance.'* (NASB)

Isaiah's reference to Assyria is not to the modern nation state of Syria, but to most of the Middle East, which once belonged to the great Assyrian Empire. The following map shows the ancient boundaries of this empire and the modern nations that were once part of it.

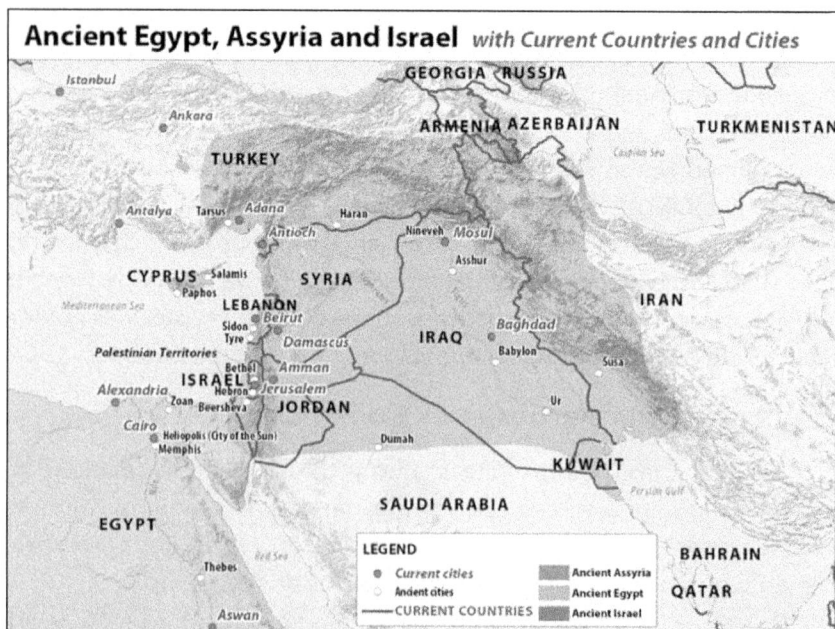

Ancient Egypt, Assyria and Israel *with Current Countries and Cities*

Used by permission from © Tom Craig, February 2010

Proclaiming Isaiah 19 in Iraq

In 2001, the Lord sent me on a prayer assignment to Iraq during the reign of Saddam Hussein, when American citizens were not exactly welcomed there. But the Lord miraculously opened the doors, and I went to Iraq by faith. In a Baghdad hotel, seated among many Middle Eastern men, I found myself across the breakfast table from an Egyptian who not only spoke English well, but was also a Spirit-filled Christian who helped lead an intercessory prayer movement in Egypt. I asked him if we could go outside to speak privately.

When I explained to my new Egyptian friend that I was not only American, but lived in Israel, his eyes opened wide as he exclaimed: "Really? It's dangerous for you to be here. Why are you here?"

"Have you heard of Isaiah 19?" I replied.

He said, "Of course, I'm an Egyptian, and that chapter is a very important prophecy about Egypt."

I explained that the Lord had told me to proclaim in ancient Nineveh (Assyria's long-time capital), Babylon and Ur that a season was beginning when the Lord would start to fulfill Isaiah 19:23–25.

"Really?" my Egyptian friend exclaimed. "The Lord told me the exact same thing, and to do it in the exact same cities!" So we prayed together onsite in Nineveh, Babylon, and Ur, proclaiming the wonderful prophecy the Lord had given Isaiah.

As our relationship has grown over the years, we have collaborated closely in ministry in Egypt. My friend became the leader of a prayer movement in Egypt that brought together literally tens of thousands of intercessors to pray for their nation.

Significance of the Isaiah 19 Highway

Why is this Isaiah 19 passage so important for our generation, and how is the Lord beginning to fulfill it? Here are some principles that can help us understand and pray into what the Lord is doing:

1. *All Nations (Ethnic Groups) Have a Unique Gift and Call from God.* When we first moved overseas for ministry in 1983, I remember

thinking (to be honest): "Why do they do things so differently here in Europe? Why don't they do them the 'right' way, like we do in America"? After a year, we'd adapted to the European way of doing things, and then I found myself thinking: "Why don't Americans do things the right way, like they do here in Europe?" I so wanted to adapt culturally, that it became hard for me to admit I was an American. Then I began to spiritualize things, saying, "I'm not an American. I'm a citizen of the Kingdom of God."

While that sounds really spiritual, it's not totally correct biblically. Yes, there is common agreement that Kingdom of God cultures surpass all human cultures in terms of such characteristics as forgiveness, humility, servanthood, etc. *But the Kingdom of God culture does not erase ethnic cultures—it redeems them.* By the work of the Holy Spirit and the blood of Jesus, we become aware of demonic influences added to our ethnic cultures that defile them and us. But once that demonic overlay is stripped away, we find that each nation (in Greek, *ethnos*, or "ethnic group") has its own distinct gifts and callings from God.

Even after the millennium, in the New Jerusalem, ethnic identities are not erased, but are given in worship to the Lord. In Revelation 21:22-27, the Apostle John said,

*22 I did not see a temple in the city, because the Lord God Almighty and the Lamb are its temple. 23 The city does not need the sun or the moon to shine on it, for the glory of God gives it light, and the Lamb is its lamp. 24 The nations will walk by its light, and the kings of the earth will bring their splendor into it. 25 On no day will its gates ever be shut, for there will be no night there. 26 **The glory and honor of the nations will be brought into it**. 27 Nothing impure will ever enter it, nor will anyone who does what is shameful or deceitful, but only those whose names are written in the Lamb's book of life.* (emphasis added)

2. To Know God Fully, We Must Know His Heart for All Abraham's Descendants. When we first moved to Jerusalem, people tried to get me to take sides against others. Some presented arguments that made you think you had to hate the Jews if you loved the Arabs, or hate the Arabs if you loved the Jews. But that is a very fleshly way of looking at the situation.

Soon after arriving, my friend John Dawson invited me to a meeting of Jewish messianic and Arab Christian pastors who were seeking deeper unity. One Arab leader shared something very simple, yet profound. He said: "If you love the Arabs with a 'soulish' love (by that, he meant a love growing out of hearing stories, seeing films, television news, etc.), then you will hate the Jews. And if you love the Jews with a 'soulish' love, then you will hate the Arabs. However, if you love either group with a spiritual love given by God, then you will love the other group."

That made a very complicated situation much simpler, because it brought us to our knees to ask the Lord for His love and His heart for all the descendants of Abraham. This in no way takes away from the truths of His unique calling upon Israel, but it helps us see that the Lord also has a wonderful destiny for the Arab peoples, and that we are to love both groups with His love.

Once I was complaining to the Lord about the Arabs having so much money from oil. I felt He rebuked me, saying that He was the one who had blessed them with wealth because of His promise to Abraham to bless the descendants of Ishmael.

In Genesis 17, when the Lord made clear that His covenant promises of salvation and His covenant regarding the Land would be made through the line of Isaac, Abraham expressed his great love for Ishmael and asked the Lord: *"If only Ishmael might live under your blessing!"* (Genesis 17:18). The Lord reaffirmed that His salvation and Land covenants would be through the line of Isaac, but He pronounced a strong prophetic blessing over Ishmael and his descendants:

20 And as for Ishmael, I have heard you: I will surely bless him; I will make him fruitful and will greatly increase his numbers. He will be the father of twelve rulers, and I will make him into a great nation. 21 But My covenant I will establish with Isaac. (Genesis 17:20–21a)

In many nations in the Middle East, I have seen, and indigenous leaders have confirmed that when a Muslim comes to the Lord, he or she almost always receives a heart revelation of God's love for the Jewish people and Israel a short time afterwards.

At our youth conference ELAV, I once asked a Muslim-background young lady believer to give her testimony of healing from leukemia. She replied: "Yes, but only if I can share the even greater testimony."

When I asked what that was, she replied, "My testimony of how the Lord gave me a love for the Jewish people and Israel."

She shared how she had been a member of Hamas, a militant Islamic terror organization. Someone from our ministry had brought food and clothing to help her family, as they were neighbors in need. Her mother was very ill at the time, and the people from our ministry prayed with her in the name of Jesus. The mother was healed and gave her life to the Lord. Her daughter was very embarrassed that her mother had become a Christian.

But later, when the daughter was diagnosed with leukemia, and told she had only a few months to live, she began to question. She told a friend at school: "I don't know whether to pray in the Muslim way or the Christian way, because when the Christians prayed, my mother was healed."

Her Muslim school friend said: "Why don't you pray that the One Who created you will reveal Himself to you and heal you? And Whoever does that, I will also serve Him."

That night the Lord Jesus came in a dream to this young woman, shining brightly, and said to her: "I am the One Who created you, and I am healing you. Go back to the doctors and they will find you are healed."

She went back to the doctors and kept insisting they take new tests, until they finally gave in and were shocked to find that she was free from leukemia! But even after this great miracle, this young woman said the greater miracle was that, when she gave her heart to Jesus, He filled it with a love for the Jewish people and for Israel!

A young Jewish messianic believer who was serving in the army also asked to testify. He said he had to serve in situations where he and his friends were attacked by Arab terrorists. He did not realize that he had allowed bitterness and prejudice to come into his heart for all Arabs. An Arab brother also shared his testimony at our conference of how Jesus had changed his heart, and had broken through the stoniness of his heart to cause him to love Jews. As the Arab brother shared, the Jewish young man suddenly was convicted by the Holy Spirit of hardening his heart and allowing in hatred toward Arabs. He said the Lord broke his heart and gave him a love for Arabs.

These are the kind of moves the Lord is doing all over the Isaiah 19 highway region of the Middle East and North Africa.

At a meeting in Egypt, we heard the testimony of a young woman coming out of a Coptic background. She explained that when she had a life-changing salvation experience, she began spending time in the Bible and with the Lord every evening in her bedroom. One night, Jesus walked into the room. She said it was not a vision, but that He actually appeared to her! He said to her: "I want you to love My people, Israel." She replied honestly, "Oh, I can't do that. I am an Egyptian, and we hate Israelis."

She said His eyes filled with tears, and He began crying. He said, "After all I have forgiven you, and the way I love you, can you not love My brothers after the flesh?" Immediately, she repented, and He flooded her heart with a love for the Jewish people and Israel.

Who knows how many hundreds or even thousands of times such revelations are being poured out across this region, as the fulfillment of Isaiah 19:23–25, a highway of reconciliation, begins?

> To pray effectively for the fulfillment of Isaiah 19, we often need our minds cleansed from prejudices produced by biased media or political opinions.

3. Our Thinking Must be Formed by God's Word, not Humanistic Media. To receive the Lord's heart for all the descendants of Abraham, and to pray effectively for the fulfillment of Isaiah 19, we often need our minds cleansed from prejudices produced by biased media or political opinions. We need to realize that the vast majority of the media worldwide are at best humanistic in their thinking, and at worst, have anti-Christ and anti-God biases.

We need to continually heed Paul's admonition: *"Do not conform to the pattern of this world, but be transformed by the renewing of your mind. Then you will be able to test and approve what God's will is—His good, pleasing and perfect will"* (Romans 12:2).

For our thoughts to be renewed and transformed by the scriptures, we should take those scriptures literally. I will not go into depth here (you can easily research this), but false teachings called "replacement theology" and "allegorical interpretation," developed primarily in the third century, have caused many to replace the word "Israel" in the Bible with the "Church" in a way that distorts the scriptures. As one example, most adherents interpret the story of the dry bones coming to life in Ezekiel 37 as referring to the Church only. Of course, it can be applied at times to the Church; but the original and primary meaning is clearly the literal Israel, as Ezekiel 37:11–14 says:

> *11 Then he said to me: "Son of man, **these bones are the people of Israel**. They say, 'Our bones are dried up and our hope is gone; we are cut off.' 12 Therefore prophesy and say to them, 'This is what the Sovereign LORD says: My people, I am going to open your graves and bring you up from them; **I will bring you back to the land of Israel**. 13 Then you, My people, will know that I am the Lord when I open your graves and bring you up from them. 14 I will put My Spirit in you and you will live, and I will settle you in your own land. Then you will know that I the LORD have spoken, and I have done it, declares the Lord.'"* (emphasis added)

If we believe that Isaiah 19:23–25 literally speaks of a great harvest springing up in Egypt and the Middle East, then we also must believe that it refers to the literal Israel in that same passage.[6] When Isaiah received this prophecy, the Egyptian and Assyrian Empires had a long history of war with each other, and with a very literal Israel invaded often by each of them.

The Heart of the Battle Is for Worship

The bottom line of the Middle East conflict is the spiritual battle for Jerusalem; in Jerusalem, it is the spiritual battle for the Temple Mount; and on the Temple Mount, the spiritual battle is for who will reign and who be worshipped on God's "holy hill."

Soon after we moved to Jerusalem, I realized that the Middle East conflict could not be understood merely in terms of human history, wars, and refugees. The spiritual dimension is pre-eminent here. I knew that *"our struggle is not against flesh and blood, but against the rulers, against the authorities, against the powers of this dark world and against the spiritual forces of evil in the heavenly realms"* (Ephesians 6:12). But as I cried out to the Lord for deeper understanding of this spiritual battle, I soon recognized that at the very center of the spiritual battle of the entire universe is the battle for worship. That is why the restoration of the Tabernacle of David as to its worship, and why the worship mentioned in Isaiah 19 are central to what the Lord is doing today in the Middle East.

> At the very center of the spiritual battle of the entire universe is the battle for worship.

And I recognized that the focal point of this universal battle is a hill that's not very impressive as a mountain—the Temple Mount. Why would such a small "hill" as the Temple Mount be the center of so much attention in both the physical and spiritual realms? It is because God's chose this lowly (for now) place as the central point for the final

---

6 For more, see Tom Craig's book: *Living Fully for the Fulfillment of Isaiah 19: When Egypt, Assyria and Israel Will Become a Blessing in the Midst of the Earth* (www.amazon.com/dp/B00J2FAKLI/).

establishment of His government on earth. As the prophet Ezekiel states:

> 1 Then the man brought me to the gate facing east, 2 and I saw the glory of the God of Israel coming from the east. His voice was like the roar of rushing waters, and the land was radiant with His glory. 3 The vision I saw was like the vision I had seen when He came to destroy the city and like the visions I had seen by the Kebar River, and I fell facedown. 4 The glory of the Lord entered the temple through the gate facing east. 5 Then the Spirit lifted me up and brought me into the inner court, and the glory of the Lord filled the temple. 6 While the man was standing beside me, **I heard Someone speaking to me from inside the temple. 7 He said:** "Son of man, this is the place of My throne and the place for the soles of My feet. This is where I will live among the Israelites forever.** (Ezekiel 43:1–7a; emphasis added)

Not only has the Lord established the Temple Mount as the "footstool" of His throne on the earth (see Isaiah 66:1), He also said: "I have installed My king on Zion, My holy mountain" (Psalm 2:6). In other words, when Jesus returns, during His millennial reign He will sit enthroned on what we now know as the Temple Mount. This is further explained in Isaiah 2:1–4:

> 1 This is what Isaiah son of Amoz saw concerning Judah and Jerusalem: 2 **In the last days the mountain of the Lord's temple will be established as the highest of the mountains; it will be exalted above the hills, and all nations will stream to it. 3 Many peoples will come and say,** "Come, let us go up to the mountain of the Lord, to the temple of the God of Jacob. He will teach us His ways, so that we may walk in His paths." The law will go out from Zion, the word of the Lord from Jerusalem. 4 He will judge between the nations and will settle disputes for many peoples.** They will beat their swords into plowshares and their spears into pruning hooks.

Nation will not take up sword against nation, nor will they train for war anymore. (emphasis added)

In view of these prophetic scriptures, it's no wonder Satan is also making the Temple Mount the focal point of his battle. He seeks to bring the nations against the very purposes of God that will be fulfilled on that "holy hill" and that signal his impending judgment.

Satan's desires concerning the Temple Mount are clear in Isaiah 14. Almost all Bible teachers agree that verse 13 speaks about Satan: "**You said in your heart, 'I will ascend to the heavens; I will sit enthroned on the mount of assembly'**" (emphasis added). The "mount of assembly" is another title of the Temple Mount, as that was where the Israelites assembled to worship.

It's clear that Satan not only covets God's throne in the heavens, *but also* God's throne on the earth. He covets God's worship in heaven *and* God's worship on earth. And Satan's covetous gaze is fixed on the Temple Mount as the center of God's throne and worship on planet Earth.

It's a sad fact that some militant Muslims are more aware of the Temple Mount being "the throne of the world" than most Christians. This is clear in a statement Hamas leader Khaled Mashal made at a Damascus mosque in 2006: "By Allah, you will be defeated. You will be defeated in Palestine. True, it is Israel that is being defeated there, but when Israel is defeated, its path is defeated, and the cowards who hide behind it are defeated ... **tomorrow, our nation [referring to Islam] will sit on the throne of the world**. This is not a figment of the imagination, but a fact." (emphasis added)

As a counterfeit to the Isaiah 19 highway, Satan is stirring up a vision for highways to Jerusalem to facilitate death and destruction. An Egyptian intercessor sent me a video of over a million Egyptians in Tahrir Square shouting that they must march to Jerusalem and lay down their lives to "liberate" it.

This fixation on Jerusalem is also at the heart of a statement ISIS militant Abu Saffiya made in a YouTube video: "Abu Bakr al-Baghdadi [former ISIS leader] says, 'God will break all barriers ... Iraq, Jordan, Lebanon ... all of them until we reach Al Quds [Jerusalem]."

The building up of these demonic "highways" to Jerusalem and the Temple Mount can be very distressing unless we realize that the Lord already foresaw and prepared a plan 700 years before Christ and revealed it to His prophet Isaiah.

4. *The Isaiah 19 Highway is Key to Restoring the Worship of the One True God to His Holy Hill in Jerusalem.* Some 2,750 years ago, the Lord had already announced His plans for His great end-time highway to Jerusalem and the foot of His throne! And as mentioned, His divine plan includes Egypt, Israel, and most of the Middle East, as Isaiah 19:23–25 says.

I believe the infrastructure of the Isaiah 19 highway is formed of houses of prayer; Isaiah makes clear in this chapter that it is a highway of *worship*.

Counterfeit Highways

On 23 September 2015, I had a vision at Succat Hallel that gives us a glimpse into what is happening in the spiritual realm in the Isaiah 19 nations.

First, I saw demonic counterfeit highways to Jerusalem under construction. These demonic highways seemed to be built quickly. There were demons driving steamrollers and laying down asphalt. At times, they ran over people and killed them, but they just poured asphalt on the dead bodies to hide them, and rolled on, seeking to finish their highways to Jerusalem.

But then I saw into the heavenlies over the Isaiah 19 region. Each house of prayer in the region was a pillar helping to hold up what was truly a *high* way first being built in the heavenlies before it would be lowered onto the earth. From each of these house-of-prayer pillars were ramps going down to earth, and angels descending and ascending like flames of fire, bringing the fire of the Holy Spirit down into the cities where these houses of prayer were located. The angels were also forming some of the houses of prayer into "houses of refuge" and some cities into "cities of refuge" that would help protect believers and the harvest in times of shaking.

I even saw some houses of prayer/refuge and cities of refuge on a map. Although I sensed it was not limited to those cities I knew, I saw them in Erbil, Iraq; Gaziantep and Diyarbakir, Turkey; Beirut, Lebanon; Jerusalem and Tiberius, Israel; Jericho; and many places in Egypt, but especially houses of prayer with a facility in the desert.

Where these heavenly highways converged over Jerusalem, I saw four pillars to the north, south, east, and west. These house-of-prayer pillars were helping hold up a ring or beltway around the city, and angelic flames of fire went faster and faster around that beltway.

Then I saw the Lord begin to judge the demonic highways to Jerusalem. The Lord put barriers around the houses and cities of refuge to protect them from demonic plans. He then sent earthquakes and tremors that began breaking up sections of the demonic highways. He sent division on the demonic armies marching on these highways, and they started fighting one another.

During these times of shaking, the angelic flames on the heavenly Isaiah 19 highway began moving more quickly over that highway, causing an acceleration of the Lord's purposes. I realized that whole sections of the Isaiah 19 highway could be lowered to the earth at any time.

Since 2008, we, along with one of our key leaders, Gary Klein, have been conducting "Birthing Houses of Prayer" seminars in many nations of the Middle East. Gary helps oversee the sending of individuals and teams of Jewish messianic,

> **Through His houses of prayer, the Lord Himself is building His House and His highways, and what once seemed impossible is happening in Egypt, Israel, and the Middle East.**

Arab, and international believers to houses of prayer in the region to strengthen them.

We realize we're only part of what the Lord is doing in the region, but we can say firsthand that He is building the Isaiah 19 highway of worship and sending forth His angels as flames of fire to aid in the building. As a result, and as the vision unfolds, we see rapidly increasing movement along this highway.

Through His houses of prayer, the Lord Himself is building His House and His highways, and what once seemed impossible is happening in Egypt, Israel, and the Middle East. Houses of prayer are being birthed and built that the Lord will use to bring great change to the cities and nations of this region, which many consider the most difficult, if not impossible region in which to see major breakthrough and change. He *will* fulfill His Word. He *will* build His highway!

CHAPTER 17

The Extended Isaiah 19 Highway

As we became increasingly involved on the Isaiah 19 highway, the Lord revealed two more major pieces of the puzzle—highway extensions from the Far East and Africa that will release large numbers of worshippers and intercessors to labor among the nations of the Isaiah 19 highway. These will serve in houses of prayer and the ingathering of the coming great harvest.

The Lord spoke to me through Jeremiah 6:16 to *"stand at the*

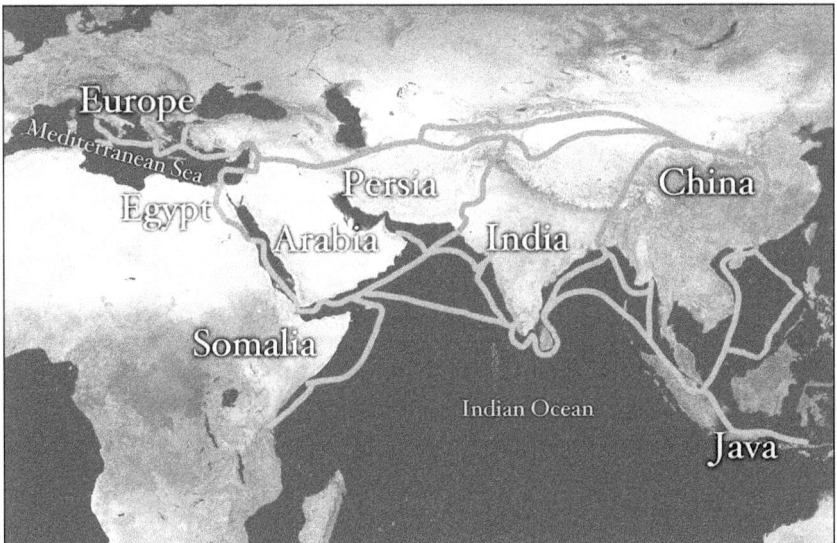

Ancient Trade Routes

crossroads and look; ask for the ancient paths". I realize this verse in its first application speaks to ancient paths of righteousness, but

> **Highway extensions from the Far East and Africa will release large numbers of worshippers and intercessors to labor among the nations of the Isaiah 19 highway.**

the Lord also stirred me to check out the ancient highways once connected to the Isaiah 19 region. It's interesting that the ancient trade routes of East Asia and Africa both converged toward Egypt, Israel, and Assyria.

The silks, spices, and incense brought from the Far East along the ancient Silk Road, and the maritime Spice and Incense Routes were highly prized and valued by the cultured cities of Israel, Greece, and Rome. Because of the dangers from raiding parties of thieves over land, and pirates attacking and sinking ships on the maritime routes, the silks, spices, and incense that did make it through to the Mediterranean countries were considered extremely valuable. This is why the frankincense and myrrh brought by the wise men from the East were gifts as valuable as the gold they also brought.

The Bible makes it clear that the incense burned on the altar of incense before the Lord in the Tabernacle of Moses, and later in the Temple of Solomon and the Second Temple was truly a "sacrifice" of treasured ingredients unto the Lord.

The recipe for the incense offered before the Lord is described in Exodus 30:34–37:

> *34 Then the LORD said to Moses, 'Take fragrant spices— gum resin, onycha and galbanum—and pure frankincense, all in equal amounts, 35 and make a fragrant blend of incense, the work of a perfumer. It is to be salted and pure and sacred. 36 Grind some of it to powder and place it in front of the Ark of the Covenant in the tent of meeting, where I will meet with you.*

It shall be most holy to you. 37 Do not make any incense with this formula for yourselves; consider it holy to the LORD.

According to the Temple incense recipe as described in the Talmud, at least some of the spices used in the incense offering came from the Far East, including the islands of Indonesia, which are sometimes called "The Spice Islands."

I can almost imagine Yeshua walking into the Temple in Jerusalem, smelling that beautiful incense and thinking, "Someday that will become the incense of worship coming from the people of Indonesia and the Far East."

Both myrrh and nard are mentioned in a romantic, intimate way in Song of Songs 4:13–14 and 5:5;13. And the perfume poured out on the feet of Yeshua in worship by Mary in Bethany (see John 12:1–10) was made from nard, a flower found in the high Himalayas of India, Nepal, and China. Again, it's easy to imagine Yeshua knowing that someday that same intimate worship would be poured out on Him from Indians, Nepalese, and Chinese.

A Call to the Far East

I had two detailed visions describing the strategic importance of believers from the Far East in building up houses of prayer and helping transform the nations mentioned in Isaiah 19:

First Asia Vision: A Giant Eagle. In 2009, I was in the spirit during worship at Succat Hallel, when I saw a giant eagle come and look very intently into my eyes. It then took me on its back to fly over Asia to see it from a higher vantage point. I first saw the Great Wall of **China**, as portions of it began to sink into the ground, indicating the Lord would open up a greater freedom for the Chinese believers to be sent out to His work in the nations. Next, I saw angels opening trapdoors to reveal tunnels beneath the earth. Angels were escorting believers down into these tunnels, where they were then given new clothing, passports, and money. The angels led them through the tunnels to an exit above ground, where they caught planes to Central Asia and the Middle East to staff new houses of prayer coming forth. Then I saw Chinese people dancing under a dragon costume, and I knew it meant they were under the influence of a dragon-like demonic power. But then the Lord reached down and lifted the dragon costume off the dancers, indicating deliverance from the power of this evil spirit. I then saw the same kind of dragon dance and deliverance from its power happening in the streets of **Taiwan**.

As we flew over **Hong Kong**, I saw very tall buildings shrinking, and I knew it represented financial reverses for many who had worshipped at the altar of materialism. However, at the same time, new skyscrapers were rising up that were made of bricks of gold. I knew these represented the businesses of believers with a vision for Kingdom of God finance, and that the gold showed they were building with that which was lasting, rather than temporal.

I then saw similar events happening in **Singapore**, and bridges being built between Hong Kong and Singapore, with the bricks of gold flowing in both directions. I believe this represented divine linking between Kingdom businesses in Singapore and in Hong Kong. Those from Hong Kong and Singapore were throwing gold bricks toward the West, which I understood to be provision for the houses of prayer and workers in Central Asia, the Middle East, and Israel. And yet their "Kingdom of God skyscrapers" kept growing higher.

Then in **Korea**, I saw North Korea and South Korea like horse shoe magnets, with the ends of the magnets facing the border and repelling one another. But the magnet over South Korea was flipped over, and now the two magnets were attracted to each other, and joined together at the border. Then the barbed wire of the border began to melt away. Almost immediately, I saw the hand of the Lord holding the two magnets together in an upright position. He used the magnets to pick up Korean believers and drop them from the magnets into various Central Asian, Middle Eastern, and North African nations to place them in new houses of prayer springing up. If South Korea is already impacting the Middle East, how much more will a re-united Korea.

Next I saw **Indonesia**. Several huge elephants were lying on their sides over the nation. When they stood up, they began to take very large logs and put them in place to build a strong swing bridge of rope and the logs. The bridge reached over into Central Asia and the Middle East. Then large numbers of Indonesians began to travel over this bridge to be part of new houses of prayer coming forth in Central Asia and the Middle East.

Next, I saw angels taking the map of **India** by the outward edges, and lifting it up and down like a giant silk canopy billowing in the hands of dancers. As India was shaken by these angels, some believers were launched from India like missiles, while others were launched like doves, again into Central Asia and the Middle East.

Later, I saw believers in the **Philippines** dressed as servants in black and white uniforms. I knew they were being used to infiltrate key homes of government and business leaders, as well as to help houses of prayer and revival being birthed, particularly in the Middle East.

An End-Time Army

On 28 December 2009, I heard: "Now is the time for the prepared arrows of the Far East to come out of the quiver, and pierce the hearts of the King's enemies." I felt this was a reference to both Psalm 45:5 and Isaiah 49:2. My attention was also drawn to Psalm 110:3 which speaks of the day of His power, when the Messiah will receive His young men like dew from the *"womb of the dawn"*.

The *"womb of the dawn"* refers to the place where the sun first rises in the morning—the Far East. I believe Psalm 110:3 refers to a huge, spiritual end-time army that the Lord will raise up from the Far East to play a great role in preparing the way for the King of

> I believe Psalm 110:3 refers to a huge, spiritual end-time army that the Lord will raise up from the Far East to play a great role in preparing the way for the King of Glory's return to Jerusalem.

> I saw a huge army of intercessors, worshippers, and harvesters coming from the Far East to help the houses of prayer in the Middle East.

Glory's return to Jerusalem. May the last-days army of the Far East be taken out of the Lord's quiver to be shot by Him into houses of prayer in Central Asia, the Middle East, and North Africa. May they embrace their key role to release the harvest in these dry and needy nations. And may they truly prepare the way of the King so that His glory may return from the East, and once again be revealed in Jerusalem.

Second Asia Vision: Horses, Camels, and Elephants: In February 2012, during a watch at Succat Hallel, I had a vision that I feel reveals part of the Lord's strategy for the Far East, Israel, and the Middle East. I saw a huge army of intercessors, worshippers, and harvesters coming from the Far East to help the houses of prayer in the Middle East.

First I saw them as HORSES running from Korea, with torches of revival fire. They were able to quickly mobilize in missions, and were the first to arrive in the Middle East in large numbers.

Then I saw them as CAMELS from China and the Asian Chinese diaspora, bringing silk, priestly clothing, and financial provision for the houses of prayer in the Middle East. They moved a little more slowly than the horses, but were very persevering, indicating they would bring the gift of perseverance under persecution. They brought large quantities of living water to pour out on the Middle East.

Then I saw ELEPHANTS coming from Indonesia. They moved even more slowly, but when they moved, they made a huge impact! They built bridges to the Middle East of logs (representing strength) and ropes (representing flexibility). On their way, they also picked up other elephants (workers) from the Philippines, Malaysia, Singapore, and India. These ELEPHANTS were massive, and began to step on and crush devils and enemy strongholds across the Middle East. Their trunks were like shofars. When they blew their sound, God's enemies began to tremble. Then the ELEPHANTS stomped on the ground, causing spiritual earthquakes and an opening up of the hard ground across the Middle East. As they continued their journey on to Jerusalem, the ELEPHANTS brought huge quantities of incense and spices for the worship in Jerusalem, just as in the times of the Tabernacle and the Temple of the Old Testament.

This army that brought such change to the Middle East were especially from three nationalities: the Koreans, the Chinese, and the Indonesians. I believe that God has chosen them especially because they have persevered and overcome in the face on persecution.

One unusual confirmation of this vision came in spring 2014, when our co-laborers, John and Una Gere, who oversee the City of David prayer room connected with us, were in Samarkand, Uzbekistan. They were praying in this ancient city that was once an important stop on the Silk Road. At a local museum, they saw a drawing tracing the outlines of a mural hundreds of years old that depicted the trade on the ancient Silk Road. Amazingly, front and center were horses, camels, and an elephant!

Here is a stylistic painting of a visualization of this vision by our friend Mack McCoy, an early leader at Succat Hallel:

Of course, the main confirmation of this vision is that it is coming to pass. I have been invited to minister in major conferences in the Far East where the primary theme was raising up and sending laborers to the houses of prayer in the Middle East. In the Middle Eastern houses of prayer with which we are connected, we see a steadily increasing number of intercessors coming from the Far East, both short- and long-term.

The African Connection: Egypt's Ancient Routes

More recently, the Lord also has been highlighting to us the increasing role that many African nations will play in building the Isaiah 19 highway. It's noteworthy that just as the ancient Assyrian Empire was far greater than the modern nation of Syria, so too the ancient Egyptian Empire was far larger than the modern nation state of Egypt. Here is a map[7] showing the extent of the ancient Egyptian Empire:

---

7   Bartholomew, J. G. (John George), E.P. Dutton (Firm), and J.M. Dent & Sons. "Egyptian Empire B.C. 1450." Map. 1913. Norman B. Leventhal Map & Education Center, https://collections. leventhalmap.org/search/commonwealth:3f463745j (accessed July 12, 2019).

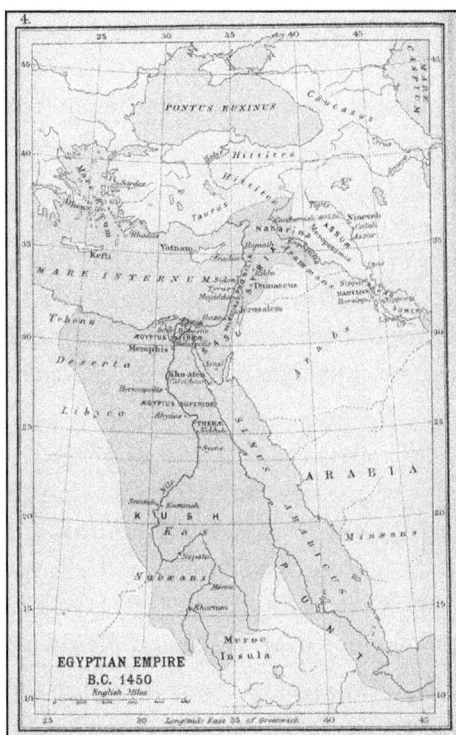

Ancient Egyptian Empire B.C.1450

Just as ancient routes in Asia connected to the Middle East, ancient routes in Africa[8] connected to Egypt, and through Egypt to the Middle East, including Israel.

Africa's Role in Rebuilding the Isaiah 19 Highway

During worship at Succat Hallel in November 2015, I saw in a vision a spotlight on Africa. The borders of Africa were enclosed by a very high wall of witchcraft and idolatry.

Then I saw the Lord strike a staff into the waters of the ocean off Cape Town, South Africa. This produced a great wave of light that swept the entire continent from South Africa to Egypt. As the wave

---

8   A visual representation of many of those routes may be seen at the following links:
     http://www.geocities.ws/ccnywciv/reader/africatrademap.jpg
     https://www.gifex.com/detail-en/2009-11-06-10899/Historical_map_of_Africa_circa_1400.
     html. According to the French map legend at the second link, the smooth black lines
     represent medieval trade routes.

progressed, there were earthquakes and shakings, and the enclosure wall of witchcraft started to crumble. Witch doctors fell on their knees to repent and to worship Jesus. Then idols began to fall.

I then saw highways of dominoes going from various points of revival and harvest in other parts of Africa, and moving in the direction of Egypt. From the south, the dominoes were falling northward from countries such as South Africa and Mozambique. From West Africa, the dominoes were falling eastward from places like Ghana, Burkina Faso, and Nigeria. As these dominoes began to fall, a momentum of revival and harvest moved through Uganda and Kenya northward and up into Ethiopia, and then into Egypt.

When the wave of light and the dominoes of harvest reached Egypt, huge, ancient idols of Egypt started to fall. I saw the Lord, as described in Isaiah 19, "riding on a swift cloud" into Egypt. Idols trembled and fell. Then a red beam of occult light coming from the Great Pyramid (which the Lord had first shown me in a vision in 1991) was extinguished, and no longer exerted influence over Egypt and the nations.

I sensed that this new level of breakthrough that was overturning witchcraft in Africa would travel from the African part of the Isaiah 19 Highway on into the Middle East, helping break through against the witchcraft in the Middle East, thus furthering that harvest as well.

This vision was soon confirmed in a remarkable way. Less than two weeks later, on 23 November, I received an email from Martin Sarvis, one of our senior leadership team, who was in South Africa at the time.

He writes: "Regarding your vision of planting the staff in the waters, and declaring a shaking that would begin to dislodge witchcraft ... I always expected I/we would be in some way involved with it physically. Instead, the Lord is obviously taking it into a much larger sphere. I felt from the beginning that it would be important to connect with someone with physical roots and authority in the land. ... Around the table the next morning [after arriving in Cape Town], I felt free to share your vision ... I made it clear that we felt the most important thing was submitting the Word to believers in Africa, whether or not we were personally to take part in the prophetic act itself. One thing that had seemed important to me was the 'staff.' I didn't feel quite right about just going out and picking up a stick somewhere. As I emphasized this, the woman [Lindy] got a look on her face, stood up and went to a closet, returning with a real 'staff'. It had been carved from almond wood by Baruch Maayan (a South African messianic Jew who currently lives in Israel). Baruch is loved and respected by the prophetic Body down here as a prophet and teacher, as well as an artist. He had made the staff in South Africa and left it with this lady when he came back to Israel. Somehow, we felt immediately that this was the staff.

"[Lindy introduced us to…] a veritable 'Deborah' named Maditshaba Moloko, a businesswoman who leased this penthouse where she believes the Lord will raise up a Prayer Room … As we spoke with her, we were blown away by her integrity and wisdom—her understanding of high-level spiritual realities over nations and regions. She also totally understood spiritual protocol, and has a keen revelation of Israel. She received the Word, and felt it to be for leaders throughout Africa to know when the act was done and be awake, alert and praying. It would also be important that Israeli leaders in Israel be participating at the same time. She also felt strongly that Baruch himself be involved, if possible, perhaps as the one to release the declaration in the water at the southernmost point off the Cape. But he had already been here last year, and no one knew when he might return.

"WELL … we prayed, sounded the shofar, etc. … and left the office, heading for the elevator. Before we got to it, out comes Maditshaba excitedly with her cell phone. She hadn't phoned or texted anyone, but at that moment she had received a text from Baruch Mayan saying he would be coming to South Africa for about a week at the end of November!"

The end result of all this was that on 11 December, several thousand African intercessors prayed in unity in different parts of Africa as Maditshaba and others joined at the edge of the waters off the Cape to worship, intercede, and make proclamations as Baruch Maayan struck the sea floor with the staff made of almond wood from Israel. They were joined by key intercessory leaders in Egypt who prayed into the vision in their nation.

Here is a stylistic painting done as a visualization of this vision by Mack McCoy, our friend and an early leader at Succat Hallel:

Vision of a Wave Across Africa Shaking Witchcraft and Idolatry and Bringing Increased Harvest by Rick Ridings

What an amazing time we live in, as we see the Lord restoring "the ancient paths" from the Far East and from Africa back into the Middle East. May the believers in these regions of the world know and act upon the mighty calling and destiny the Lord is giving them in His end-time plans.

CHAPTER 18

The Mountains of Society

In the last days the mountain of the LORD's temple will be established as the highest of the mountains.

—Isaiah 2:2

A "mountain of society" describes a specific area or pillar of culture that needs the salt and light of the Kingdom of God. These "mountains" are commonly defined as: business, government, media, arts and entertainment, education, family and religion.

I (Rick) had a vision in which I saw people striving and straining to claw their way up a mountain of society. Just as they seemed to be making progress, they suddenly lost their footing and started sliding back down; or someone else pushed them out of the way seeking to get up the mountain ahead of them.

In stark contrast, I saw others who were ascending into the third heaven through worship and prayer. There, *"seated in heavenly places in Christ Jesus"* (Ephesians 2:6 KJV), these people were receiving

> The Lord is raising up houses of prayer to become "birthing rooms", a place of intimacy with Him, where creative ideas are born that can bring change to specific areas of society.

creative ideas from the Holy Spirit, and then parachuting down onto the top of the particular "mountain"—the place and role in society—to which the Lord had called them. They were then able to have a great impact on that area of society.

Some critics of the worship and prayer movements would say that houses of prayer are a withdrawal from society. To the contrary, I believe the Lord is raising up houses of prayer to become "birthing rooms". There, in a place of intimacy with Him, creative ideas are born that can bring change to these specific areas of society. As 1 John 5:4 says, *"whatever is born of God overcomes the world"* (NKJV).

We saw this happen in Succat Hallel concerning the mountain of arts and entertainment. One of our worship leaders shared with me (Patricia) a vision to compose an oratorio (a classical piece of music for orchestra and singers that tells a story), and to put on a free concert as a gift to Israel. She asked if she could do night watches, and during the quiet hours of the night she was able to create one of the most touching and powerful musical love stories I have ever heard.

Night after night she labored to birth this work of art. She meditated on Old Testament scriptures and carefully crafted the songs in the worshipful atmosphere that can only be found in a place that is solely set apart for 24/7 worship and prayer. The Lord increased her love for Israelis as she diligently sought to create a work that would draw them to the Lover of their souls. What came forth was a beautifully crafted musical work using many of the scriptures from Song of Songs, as well as Isaiah 53.

Now she had to pray for a choir and an orchestra to sing and play her work. Back to the night watch she went to seek the Lord. He told her to go to the classiest and most expensive hotel in the city—the famous King David Hotel—for a Passover meal. She entered the dining room and sat at the back table. Soon a man entered the room, happened to notice her sitting alone, and invited her to come sit at a place of honor at the head table near the orchestra.

As she talked further with him, she learned that he was the conductor of an orchestra, and he offered to help her find top quality musicians and singers! She raised the money to rent a large hall, and the concert was a resounding success. Succat Hallel volunteers were the ushers for this event. The vast majority of the large audience was Israeli. We sat in the midst of many Israelis who sat mesmerized by the music with tears streaming down their faces, as they heard their scriptures put to lovely, anointed melodies.

Called to Permeate Society

From very early on in Succat Hallel, one of our mandates has been to provide a safe place for people with a calling to pray for a particular mountain of society to lead or be part of a watch for that purpose. For example, for several years, we had a businessman who prayed for Jewish messianic owners of businesses in Israel. This is very key to the fulfillment of the prophetic scriptures that say the Lord will pour out His blessings on those Jews called to live in their ancestral homeland. Without financial provision, it is impossible for people to be able to live here. As this businessman prayed over Jewish men and women in business, word began to get around, and people started coming from some distance away. One person even drove an hour and a half each way to be built up and inspired by this time of prayer. Some said that they had not been able to find such uplifting fellowship elsewhere.

Those called to a particular mountain of society need a lot of encouragement. One of the purposes of prophecy, according to 1 Corinthians 14:3, is to build up and encourage us. As one brother said, "If the people in your church are not encouraged, perhaps there needs to be more prophecy." And prophecy often comes forth from the house of prayer.

About fifteen years ago, I (Rick) was at a gathering of messianic pastors and leaders in Israel. During the prayers, the Lord gave me a prophetic word for a young man who was beginning to practice law. I saw that he was like a David, and had to be careful not to take on "Saul's armor" (see 1 Samuel 17:38–39) of trusting only in his legal knowledge, but to worship and depend on the Lord—like David did in order to bring down Goliath at the right time. He said the prophecy was almost word for word like one given to him almost ten years before. At a key moment, he asked if he could come to Succat Hallel to share about a particular "giant" he was facing, and to receive prayer. He has since won a case on behalf of believers at the Supreme Court level, and is having an impact on spiritual lawfare (spiritual battles taking place in courts of law) in other nations as well. But he needed the prophetic encouragement coming from the house of prayer.

The other side of this coin is that we in the houses of prayer need to keep "real" and in touch with daily life outside our context in order to be most effective in our prayers. We believe it's important for those with a specialized calling of worship or intercession to have the possibility through "mountains of society" prayer watches to keep in touch with the daily reality faced by those called to these areas of society.

Sometimes a house of prayer is called to focus on one specific mountain of society. I believe that creative new expressions will be birthed in such houses of prayer. They also provide a venue in which believers called to influence a specific area of society may be refreshed, encouraged, inspired, and find others with the same calling.

Patricia and I have had the privilege of praying a prayer of dedication for two such houses of prayer in America: The Hollywood House of Prayer, led by our friends Jonathan and Sharon Ngai; and "David's Tent", a Washington D.C. house of prayer led by our friends Jason and Kimberlee Hershey.

The Hollywood House of Prayer's first main facility was a large room that had been part of a studio that had produced hit television programs for over forty years. This key location provided access and relationships with those in the media. They work closely with a local church that has over nine hundred members working in some aspect of the media. It is a "salt shaker" that is not isolated from society, but is able to be "salt and light" in a very dark setting.

David's Tent, the Washington D.C. House of Prayer, is called to worship in the very heart of the capital of the United States of America in a literal tent. With their strong worship anointing, they are changing the atmosphere in this strategic governmental location. The Lord opened the doors for them to host 24/7 worship and prayer on the

White House Ellipse for six weeks each in 2012 and 2013. They have now been conducting 24/7 worship and prayer on the Washington Mall since 11 September 2015. Only history ("His story") will reveal the effect of the Presence of the Lord manifested in the government realm through their corporate worship and intercession.

One of the key callings of the house of prayer in this season is to help bring healthy spiritual shifts towards righteousness on the mountains of society in our cities and nations.

CHAPTER 19

Watching Over the Harvest

The harvest is plentiful, but the workers are few. Ask the Lord of the harvest, therefore, to send out workers into his harvest field.
—Luke 10:2

I believe we are on the verge of the greatest harvest of people coming into the Kingdom of God in all of history. This has already begun in some parts of the world. We are called not only to pray for *"laborers for the harvest"* but also to watch over and protect that harvest in prayer.

In Israel today, one can still see ancient stone watchtowers that were built to watch over the harvest, such as the one in the photo below:

A recreated ancient harvest watchtower at Yad Hashmona, Israel [9]

Isaiah speaks of one such watchtower in a song about the Lord's vineyard: *"I will sing for the one I love a song about His vineyard: My loved one had a vineyard on a fertile hillside. He dug it up and cleared it of stones and planted it with the choicest vines. He built a watchtower in it"* (Isaiah 5:1–2).

Later, Isaiah wrote a second song about His vineyard:

> *1 In that day, the Lord will punish with His sword, His fierce, great and powerful sword, Leviathan, the gliding serpent, Leviathan, the coiling serpent; He will slay the monster of the sea. 2 ... Sing about a fruitful vineyard: 3 I, the Lord, watch over it; I guard it day and night; so that no one may harm it.* " (Isaiah 27:1–3)

The two passages above are framed as songs about His fruitful vineyard. These "songs" speak of anointed praise and worship as part of the spiritual covering of the vineyard we are given to watch over. They also allude to defending it from spiritual warfare. Thus, the watchman, and prayer for laborers for the harvest mandates converge in the house of prayer as we watch over the harvest, from seedtime to fruit.

Guarding the Seed

Jesus spoke very clearly that when the powerful seeds of the Kingdom of God are planted, the enemy will hasten to send birds to eat up that harvest and will seek to sow weeds in the fields (see Matthew 13:3–28). It is important to not allow the enemy to steal the harvest through spirits of division, selfish ambition, fear or distraction.

During the time of Gideon, Israel gave in to fear and did not rise up to protect the harvest, as we see in Judges 6:2–5:

> *2 Because the power of Midian was so oppressive, the Israelites prepared shelters for themselves in mountain clefts, caves and strongholds. 3 Whenever the Israelites planted their crops, the Midianites, Amalekites and other eastern peoples invaded the country. 4 They camped on the land and ruined the crops all the way to Gaza and did not spare a living thing for Israel, neither sheep nor cattle nor donkeys. 5 They came up with their livestock and their tents like swarms of locusts. It*

was impossible to count them or their camels; they invaded the land to ravage it.

The Jesus People Harvest

In the days of the Jesus People movement, in the summer of 1970, I (Rick) saw the Lord release a supernatural harvest in my hometown of Muskegon, Michigan. A group of young adults had been drawn together from different church backgrounds to seek the Lord in worship and prayer. One day the Lord spoke to us to take that worship out into a public place, a park near the beach in our city where many young hippies were doing drugs. To our amazement, they were very drawn to our simple worship, and started asking questions.

I recognized a young guy who had been in my high school. He told me that experimentation with marijuana had eventually led him into full-scale heroin addiction. He didn't know how to stop. I explained to him that if he would really repent and turn his life over to Jesus, that Jesus could deliver him without any "cold turkey" (severe symptoms of withdrawal). To my great surprise, he said "Yes. I want that." He was instantly delivered without withdrawal symptoms!

He was so excited, he wanted to see his friends and those to whom he had been selling drugs come into that freedom. We would go on the beach and he would share his testimony with them, and then he would turn to me and say, "Now you tell them all that Bible stuff." For the next month, we saw at least one young person dramatically come to the Lord each day.

But then the enemy tried to stop this harvest through a spirit of fear and intimidation. The drug dealer who had been over my friend sent word that we were ruining his business, and warned that if we showed up on the beach again, he would have us killed. But we cried out to the Lord, and he delivered us from this spirit of fear. We were protected, and the harvest was not stolen.

Worship and Prayer Advance a Harvest in Algeria

Algeria is a nation in North Africa that has been ruled by Islam since its invasion hundreds of years ago. In 1987, I met a young man "Nabyle" (not his real name in order to protect him) from the mountainous Berber region of Algeria called Kabylie. At that time he was one of only five Muslim-background Christian believers in that whole region, and he had left for Belgium. Having been driven away by the intense persecution, he was attending a Bible college when I met him. He did not intend to return to Algeria. The Lord gave me a word of knowledge for him in a chapel service at which I was speaking. He said it was very true for him, and we became friends, as he had a deep desire to grow in worship.

Later on, he returned to Algeria. He felt the Lord told him he was not to try to evangelize right away, but to find at least one of the four other believers who would commit to worship and pray with him all night every Friday night. He only found one who was willing, and they became a "house of prayer" of two persons!

After six months of worshipping and praying together all night every Friday, the Lord spoke a clear strategy to them. They felt the Lord told them that the primary opposition in Kabylie was not from the Muslim religion, but from spirits of witchcraft, which was very prevalent. They felt the Lord told them to proclaim (covered by the blood of Jesus) that the Lord would expose and root out witchcraft from their region.

Soon after they made this proclamation, a witch was discovered trying to kill a baby in an occult ceremony. The region was shocked. They had thought that it was only "white magic" and not "black magic" being practiced among them. Because they are a very family-oriented culture, there was a great outcry, and almost all the witches either stopped witchcraft or moved out of the region.

Almost immediately miracles started, and the harvest began to come in. "Nabyle" prayed over his paralyzed sister in the name of Jesus. She immediately got up and started running around the house screaming; "I've been healed by the name of Jesus!" Her father, who was a leader in the village mosque, was so happy she was healed, but not happy that it was "in the name of Jesus"!

An accelerated harvest began. I saw firsthand in visits there that something extraordinary had been released. People started having visions and dreams. One whole village had the same dream about Jesus on the same night. Many were healed, and I know firsthand of at least one who was raised from the dead. Within about ten years, they had grown from five believers to over ten thousand believers in their region!

And it all started through a small "restoration of the Tabernacle of David", as two young men committed to worship and pray all night every Friday.

Reaping the Harvest Fields of Indonesia

I also have witnessed with my own eyes a great harvest in Indonesia, the country with the largest Muslim population of any nation in the world. Not long ago, many churches were being burned down in Indonesia, and the percentage of Christians was very low. But now, thousands of Muslims are coming to the Lord.

I have had the privilege of ministering at conferences of the national prayer movement there, and for the leadership of one of their largest churches. On one island where I spoke at a pastors' conference, one of the leaders told me just six months later that over thirty thousand Muslims had come to the Lord in those six months on their island alone!

Daniel Pandji, Tony Mulia, and other leaders who have become friends all told me that they feel the great breakthrough in harvest can be traced to one thing: the multiplication of houses of prayer (which they call "prayer towers".)

One radical Muslim who had been burning down church buildings and persecuting believers had a miraculous, Saul-of-Tarsus-type encounter with Jesus. Around 2004, he was led to begin a house of prayer. Within a few years, it had grown to about seventeen houses of prayer in the Jakarta area, of which four were 24/7.

Within a short time, there was an explosive growth of the Body of Christ in areas of Indonesia. A real outpouring of healings, signs and wonders began. Churches started multiplying. Believers even came into important government positions (though not without persecution). And the nation of Indonesia is now experiencing major change and transformation. That growth continues to be fueled by the houses of prayer, which have continued to multiply as well.

One evidence of the great harvest in Indonesia was a prayer meeting of over 120,000 believers in the largest stadium of the capital, Jakarta, during the World Prayer Assembly in May 2012. What a privilege it was to witness that gathering, to look out on that sea of believers, and hear them singing: "The Whole Earth is Filled with Your Glory". It was estimated that another 2 million Indonesian believers took part in that stadium prayer via satellite video linkups.

Why Did So Many Past Revivals Wane?

One encouraging dynamic I've observed firsthand in revivals or moves of the Holy Spirit in areas of Indonesia and China is that these moves are still going strong after fifteen years or more. This stands in stark contrast to the history of revivals in the West, where church historians can pinpoint starting dates and basic ending years for those revivals or awakenings.

Worship and Prayer Keep the Fires Burning

What makes the difference? I believe the great emphasis on prayer and worship in the Far East provides the fuel to keep the fires burning. I believe houses of prayer are key not only to sparking change in cities and nations, but also to seeing lasting, continuing change in those cities and nations.

On a visit to Indonesia, I was asked to share at a meeting of the pastors, elders, and ministry area leaders for churches that were birthed out of the Gereja Bethel Church in greater Jakarta. Being aware of the impact of this great church, led by Pastor Niko Njotorahardjo, I thought there would be a few hundred leaders there. To my great surprise, there were over eight thousand leaders in attendance! Later that evening, when I visited their prayer tower, which is overseen by Pastor Niko's sister, our good friend Kristina, I was reminded why there seems to be no dying down of these revival fires after so many years. The worship leader, who had just led worship for over eight thousand leaders, was now in the prayer tower with about fifty other people just seeking the Lord. He was on the floor receiving refreshment from the Lord with his children next to him, who were also worshipping and praying. Those in the room ranged from children to the elderly, yet with one heart they were pouring out simple but deep worship to the Lord.

> Houses of prayer are key not only to sparking change in cities and nations, but also to seeing lasting, continuing change in those cities and nations.

One profile of Pastor Niko's ministry states: "The church started with 400 people in Jakarta, and Dr. Niko started without ... any theological background and experience as a pastor; his experience was in leading worship. As the Lord called him to be the first full-time worshipper in Indonesia, his gospel album became a phenomenon in the era of the eighties and early nineties. Almost every Sunday ... he ... [led] the congregation into praising and worshiping the Lord, and then [shared] the Word of God about praise and worship. Pastor Niko believes that the mandate entrusted to him by God is to restore 'The Tabernacle of David,' which is, Prayer, Praise & Worship in Unity, day and night."

These Indonesians are just as human as those touched in the past by the fires of spiritual awakening in the West, where the fires died down. But the difference is, these Indonesians keep coming to the house of prayer to seek the Lord in worship and prayer. And through this very simple means, the fires do not die down, but are continually refueled.

Praying Fathers

The apostle Paul was not only a great harvester, he also was a great intercessor who watched over the harvest in prayer. He wrote to the believers in Galatia: *"My dear children, for whom I am again in the pains of childbirth until Christ is formed in you"* (Galatians 4:19). Most of his epistles record that he prayed over those who were part of the harvest in the places where he had ministered.

> The apostle Paul was not only a great harvester, he also was a great intercessor who watched over the harvest in prayer.

The battle for the harvest is not finished the moment a great harvest is released. Just as with our own physical children, we must watch and pray for these spiritual children to be protected from the plans of the thief, and to come into full maturity.

PART 3

THE POWER
OF HIS
PRESENCE

CHAPTER 20

His Ways Are Higher Than Our Ways

As the heavens are higher than the earth, so are My ways higher than your ways and My thoughts than your thoughts.

—Isaiah 55:9

Sometimes circumstances go completely opposite of what we hoped or believed was best for us or our city or nation. Yet, we pray as Yeshua taught us to pray in Matthew 6:9–13 (KJV):

9 Our Father which art in Heaven, Hallowed be thy name.

10 Thy Kingdom come. Thy will be done on earth, as it is in heaven.

11 Give us this day our daily bread.

12 And forgive us our debts,
as we forgive our debtors.

13 And lead us not into temptation, but deliver us from evil;
For thine is the kingdom, and the power, and the glory forever.
Amen.

I (Patricia) think of the early disciples praying their Lord's prayer—this prayer that they heard their Master pray. But after seeing so many people healed and delivered by the hand of Yeshua, not only did their hero die—their mighty deliverer was nailed to a cursed cross and died the most humiliating and shameful death. He then surprised them by appearing to them as their resurrected Savior.

But after forty days He ascended into heaven, and left them alone to wait in an upper room for the unknown power of the Holy Spirit.

How would He come? By faith they waited and probably prayed the Lord's prayer again. They were learning that things don't always go the way they want, think or hope, but still they waited, and He did come! He came, and they received power from on high to witness and do miracles in His name.

But then one of those witnesses died a terrible, painful death by stoning. Stephen's death must have been a blow to the disciples, and they must have been tempted to run and hide, and no longer trust in their God of miracles. The Lord then miraculously saved Saul and made him a great apostle. The Lord used the very one who had been persecuting them to strengthen them in their faith, and to get them out of their hiding places and back onto the streets to testify to the power of Yeshua—the author and finisher of their faith (see Hebrews 12:2). This was another difficult test, and the tests and the miracles go on and on, hand in hand. Yet even what the enemy means for evil, the Lord turns for our good.

In 2008, we were riding a wave of blessing at Succat Hallel. By God's grace, our international staff had grown rapidly, and we had experienced over three years of 24/7 worship and prayer in our facility overlooking Mount Zion. That summer, we conducted our second successful youth conference, which brought together several hundred Jewish, Arab, and Palestinian young people. It looked like we were going *"from strength to strength."* (See Psalm 84:7)

But suddenly, our world was shaken. Patricia and I had gone away after the youth conference to rest for a few days in an apartment offered to us by ministry friends in Switzerland. We were thanking the Lord for His provision of such a peaceful place, when our main administrator contacted us with urgent news: overnight, a policy of the Ministry of the Interior of the State of Israel had changed, and we would no longer be able to get five-year volunteer visas for our staff. In fact, we would only be able to get two-year visas, and everyone who had been with us for more than two years would have to leave as soon as their current visas expired.

We were shocked. It had taken eight years to build up to a strong number of staff, and now half were going to have to leave in six months!

When Things Don't Go the Way We Expect

As I complained to the Lord about this situation, He reminded me He was either sovereign over the Ministry of the Interior and its visa policies, or He was not sovereign at all (God cannot be "partially" sovereign). The Lord reminded me that the Swiss towns down in the valley beneath the mountains where we were staying had looked very large up-close, but now looked small from the perspective of the high mountains. The Lord said to worship and "come up higher" to get His perspective on what looked to us to be such a critical situation.

As we asked for His perspective, He spoke to us that He was doing three things through this situation:

(1) He said the number of our international staff was growing too fast and, if this pace continued, we'd never have many indigenous, local staff—so He was the one who was "putting on the brakes" as to their numbers.

(2) He said He was going to "push on the accelerator" to bring in local Jewish and Arab staff.

(3) To my great surprise, especially given that I was asking how we were to "survive," He said we would not only continue to have 24/7 worship and prayer, but that we would soon be helping to establish and strengthen houses of prayer throughout the Middle East!

And those three things are exactly what He did over the next few years. But we had to learn to get His perspective and peace when things did not go the way we thought they would. We can honestly say ten years later that His ways really are higher and better than ours, and that it was well worth going through shaking to bring us into a fuller understanding of His vision, purposes, and strategy for us.

Releasing Workers to the Harvest

As I approached the Lord further about our international staff who would have to leave within six months, He impressed me with a deeper understanding in my spirit. He said: "You may either resent it when I call someone who has been with you to another place and positioning in My Kingdom, and I will not replace them—or you may choose to 'sow' them freely into My Kingdom, in which case I will not only replace them, but I will add others to you as well. As in finances, so with people: *'Give and you shall receive.'*" (see Luke 6:38).

What a release this understanding brought to my spirit! I soon saw the wisdom of His ways—a key couple moved to Alexandria, Egypt, to help "midwife" the house of prayer being birthed there through young Egyptians. And what a blessing they were there with their loving and releasing attitudes. Others who had to leave because of the visa decision also went to other houses of prayer and ministries in the Middle East. I saw that this was one way the Lord was fulfilling the surprising third statement He had given me on the Swiss mountaintop—that He would use us to help multiply houses of prayer in the Middle East.

Now when the Lord leads someone who has been with us to move on to another position in His Kingdom, it is still difficult, but I am honestly able to say: "The Lord gives and the Lord takes away, blessed be the Name of the Lord" (see Job 1:21). I am able to pray over them, "sowing" them into His Kingdom purposes, and knowing that He is the One Who will continue to provide not only finances, but also watchmen for our house of prayer.

Ever-increasing Faith

In the life and walk of Abraham, it seems the Lord required him to go from *"faith to faith"* by taking ever-increasing steps of faith. Whether it is in the area of finances, staffing, facilities, or mandates He has given us, our heavenly Father lovingly seeks to build our faith, one of the three qualities of 1 Corinthians 13:13 that last forever: faith, hope, and love.

Even at the beginning of Succat Hallel, the Lord worked in His ways that were higher than our ways. In January 2000, in response to what the Lord had told us on Mount Zion, we moved into a large, expensive apartment within walking distance of the original Tabernacle of David. A Christian businessman who had a heart for houses of prayer paid for the move and the first month's rent. But then his business went under, and we still had to pay for this huge apartment, as we had signed a lease for a year. As we prayed about it, we felt the Lord had allowed it so we would not look to and trust in one man, but look to and trust in God for our support. Someone at a watch saw a vision of many fires, and she said she felt the Lord would provide from many sources. From that moment on, we began to see the Lord provide in awesome, miraculous ways from different people in amounts that continue to amaze us!

When we first rented and renovated the City of David prayer room in 2006, it was by faith; we still didn't know how we would be able to continue to pay the rent each month for this second prayer room. We prayed for a financial miracle, and the Lord laid it on the hearts of two doctors—a husband and wife—to give almost the entire rent every month! Today, more than twelve years later, they are still providing a major portion of the rent. This has been a confirmation all these years that it was indeed God's will for us to have a second prayer room, and we continue to support one another.

The Far East Wave to the Middle East

Because His ways are higher than our ways, and His thoughts are higher than our thoughts (see Isaiah 55:9), we must learn to value His prophetic direction.

In 2009, the Lord spoke strongly to my spirit that we were to focus less on building our network of relationships in the USA and Europe, and focus more on building relationships in Asia. He spoke both in terms of worshippers and intercessors for the houses of prayer, and also of finances. He showed us that He was going to begin to use the Far East much more in the Middle East. Others on our leadership team, especially John and Una Gere, also felt this great pull toward

> Because His ways are higher than our ways, and His thoughts are higher than our thoughts (Isaiah 55:9), we must learn to value His prophetic direction.

the Far East that Patricia and I were sensing.

After a few years of walking out this prophetic direction, we saw the numbers of staff members and finances from America go down (especially after some of the economic shakings there), and the amount of finances and staff from the Far East greatly increase.

Had we not been open to His prophetic direction, we might have missed a big wave that the Lord wanted to use to move us along more quickly in the fulfillment of His promises to us.

May we as leaders of houses of prayer learn to trust the only One who sees the full picture. May we daily walk a life of faith that mirrors what we sing in worship: He is "Sovereign Over Us."

CHAPTER 21

Inquiring of the Lord

*As the eyes of servants look to the hand of their master, as the eyes
of a maid to the hand of her mistress, so our eyes look to
the Lord our God until He has mercy on us.*
—Psalm 123:2 (NKJV)

Birthing the First House of Prayer

It would be much easier on our flesh if we could receive blueprints
and formulas for starting and building a house of prayer. But the
Lord is after more than a house of prayer: He is after our hearts, and
relationship. He is building our character. And He is preparing us to
be a dwelling place for His Presence. So He purposefully keeps us in a
place of utter dependence upon Him.

King David, the first spiritual father to a house of prayer, learned this
the hard way when he first attempted to bring the ark of the covenant—
the focal point of God's manifest Presence—to the tent he had erected
for it in Jerusalem at the Lord's command.

The ark had been returned to Israel—and now God had chosen
David to bring it to Jerusalem, where God's manifest Presence was to
be placed at the center of the political, business, cultural, and even the
military life of Israel's capital city.

In the "birthing process," David correctly understood the vision—a
resting place for the ark of the covenant. However, David almost
"miscarried" during the birthing process when he thought he could
bring back the ark of the Presence through his own wisdom, power,

wealth, and strength. He set out to bring the ark back with an impressive show of fleshly strength: thirty thousand strong young men, and a new cart pulled by oxen, the equivalent of a Mercedes limousine in our day (see 2 Samuel 6:1–3).

But God was not impressed. He is impressed when we listen to His voice and obey it. The Lord was not about to allow His Presence to be brought by the strength of man. David was even angry with the Lord, and the birthing of the Tabernacle of David was delayed, until David could overcome his offense against God, and realize he had not inquired of the Lord as to how to bring in the ark of His Presence.

2 Samuel 6:6–9 records:

> 6 When they came to the threshing floor of Nakon, Uzzah reached out and took hold of the ark of God, because the oxen stumbled. 7 The Lord's anger burned against Uzzah because of his irreverent act; therefore God struck him down, and he died there beside the ark of God. 8 Then David was angry because the LORD's wrath had broken out against Uzzah, and to this day that place is called Perez Uzzah. 9 David was afraid of the LORD that day and said, "How can the ark of the Lord ever come to me?"

The Threshing Floor of Preparation

When we come to the "threshing floor," our wrong motivations and attitudes are revealed, and like chaff, are separated out. It's interesting that it is Uzzah, whose name means "strength," who is struck down after the irreverent act of trying to "save the ark" by touching it in a way prohibited in the divine instructions God had given to Moses. Those instructions required that the ark be carefully covered by the priests, and then carried via poles on the shoulders of the Levites, who were not to look on or touch the ark upon pain of death (see Exodus 25:12–15; Numbers 4:5,18–20). It is good for us to learn not to try to stabilize that which God is shaking.

We must come to the place where we are continually desperate for His Presence. *But to know God's manifest Presence, we must* first pass by the threshing floor. The threshing floor that David experienced belonged to an Israelite named Nachon—and one meaning of Nachon is "prepared."

When we come to a place of threshing in our lives, it is actually the grace of God that sifts the motives of our hearts, so we can be *prepared* to dwell in His glory, and not be consumed because of a lack of reverence for the Lord in our lives. Thus this sifting or correction shows we are His children. As Hebrews 12:5–11 says:

> **We must come to the place where we are continually desperate for His Presence. But to know God's manifest Presence, we must first pass by the threshing floor.**

5 *Have you completely forgotten this word of encouragement that addresses you as a father addresses his son? It says,*

"My son, do not make light of the Lord's discipline, and do not lose heart when He rebukes you, 6 because the Lord disciplines the one He loves, and He chastens everyone He accepts as His son."

7 Endure hardship as discipline; God is treating you as His children. For what children are not disciplined by their father? 8 If you are not disciplined … then you are not legitimate, not true sons and daughters at all. 9 Moreover, we have all had human fathers who disciplined us and we respected them for it. How much more should we submit to the Father of spirits and live! 10 They disciplined us for a little while as they thought best; but God disciplines us for our good, in order that we may share in His holiness. 11 No discipline seems pleasant at the time, but painful. Later on, however, it produces a harvest of righteousness and peace for those who have been trained by it.

Inquiring of the Lord at Every Step

Later David realized that it was his own pride and rashness that had delayed the birthing. But because he was still carrying the vision in the womb of his heart, he continued to seek God, and he eventually understood where he had done wrong the first time. In 1 Chronicles 15:12-15, David told the Levites:

> 12 *"You are the heads of the Levitical families; you and your fellow Levites are to consecrate yourselves and bring up the ark of the LORD, the God of Israel, to the place I have prepared for it.* 13 **It was because you, the Levites, did not bring it up the first time that the LORD our God broke out in anger against us. We did not inquire of Him about how to do it in the prescribed way.** *" 14 So the priests and Levites consecrated themselves in order to bring up the ark of the LORD, the God of Israel. 15 And the Levites carried the ark of God with the poles on their shoulders, as Moses had commanded in accordance with the word of the Lord* (emphasis added).

A successful birthing comes not only by receiving the right vision, but also by asking the Lord as to how and when *He* will bring the vision to pass. As David learned to seek the Lord as to how and when to bring up the ark, his changed attitudes of dependence, humility and obedience enabled him to carry the ark and the manifest Presence of God into the center of life in Israel's capital city, Jerusalem.

> A successful birthing comes not only by receiving the right vision, but also by asking the Lord as to how and when He will bring the vision to pass.

If we are to see the fulfillment of the vision the Lord has given us for the house of prayer, we too must learn to trust Him and to "inquire of Him" when things don't go the way we thought they would. Ultimately, our focus is not just to nurture the house of prayer—the baby the Lord has entrusted to our care—but in the deepest sense, it is to see the manifest Presence of the Lord coming into the center of the life of our city and nation.

David's first attempt to bring the ark of the covenant to Jerusalem is a powerful example of how we can hear from the Lord and have the right vision, yet not accomplish that vision because we are trying to do it in the power of our flesh. *We cannot bring the ark of God's manifest Presence in the power of the flesh.* The Lord does not give us a blueprint, but a relationship in which He is more than willing to communicate to us each step of the way. A house of prayer that is born of God will be built by day-by-day trust and obedience.

Discipline Learned at Father's Knee

I am adopted. When I was a boy about six years old, we lived near a river in South Dakota. Because of the danger of drowning, my adoptive father gave me very strong warnings that I was not allowed to swim in that river unless accompanied by my older brother, who was fifteen.

One day, some of my young friends wanted me to go swimming with them in the river. I went to ask permission from my parents, but I saw they were lying in bed, taking a nap. So I joined my friends, having great fun in the river. Suddenly my father appeared. He was very angry, and called me by my full name: "Richard Mark Ridings." When he used my full name, I knew I was in big trouble!

I quickly explained to my father that I had forgotten he had said I was not allowed to swim in the river without my older brother (I honestly had forgotten). My father replied: "Well then, I will help your memory." He took off his belt and applied it to the part of my anatomy that was padded for correction. It really hurt at the moment. But my memory vastly improved, and I never went swimming without my older brother again!

The wisdom and grace of my father's correction was proven soon after that when one of my little friends was swimming in the river and started sinking in some mud. He grabbed hold of a metal pipe close by, not realizing it was attached to an electric pump. He was instantly killed. I could so easily have been with him and have been electrocuted as well, if it had not been for the loving correction of my father.

My father's correction prepared me to have a good, long life. I realized when I became a father how difficult it can be to discipline your child for disobedience. But I also saw that it produces the fruit of life and righteousness in that child. And it really is a sign that your child is well-beloved.

Lessons of the Threshing Floor

The threshing floor is not a symbol of destructive judgment, but of redemptive discipline that prepares us for a good and fruitful life. In the book of Ruth, it's worth noting that it was at the threshing floor that Ruth's heart and motives were shown to be pure, and there she was brought into the first level of relationship with Boaz (see Ruth 3).

And it was at the threshing floor that King David at first reacted to the Lord's correction by taking offense against Him. Before David could successfully bring up the ark of the Lord's Presence to Jerusalem, he first had to deal with the offense in his heart toward God. David had to humble himself to "inquire of the Lord" and acknowledge that God was not at fault, but he was. He had to take responsibility for his pride and anger, and come in dependency, asking God to reveal His ways to him. *Likewise, for us to know God's manifest Presence, we must first deal with offenses toward God.*

> The threshing floor is not a symbol of destructive judgment, but of redemptive discipline that prepares us for a good and fruitful life.

How did David come to recognize the true situation? When he inquired of the Lord, God showed Him that only the consecrated Levites were to bring up the ark, as referenced above in 1 Chronicles 15:13: *"It was because you, the Levites, did not bring it up the first time that the Lord our God broke out in anger against us. We*

did not inquire of Him about how to do it in the prescribed way"
(emphasis added).

When we deal with offenses, we need to "inquire of the Lord". In His great grace, He will help us gain a larger perspective where we can see His wisdom was at work all along, even though we did not understand that at the time.

I had a lesson on this topic during our first trip behind the Iron Curtain in 1983. We were taking Bibles to believers in Poland and Czechoslovakia. After miraculously getting the Bibles into Poland, and ministering comfort to a Polish pastor who had just been released from nine months of prison with daily interrogation, we headed with great joy to the border with Czechoslovakia, where we were scheduled to minister that evening.

We had transited Czechoslovakia on our way to Poland, and I assumed it would be easy to get into that country, since we'd already gone through hours of being searched on our way in (where they did not find the Bibles), and were now entering from another communist nation. But to my great surprise, the border guard said we could not enter Czechoslovakia! He said that when we had transited on our way to Poland, the Czech border guard had torn off one too many copies of our visa, and now we did not have the copy we needed to re-enter. I asked, "So you see clearly that it was a mistake made by a border guard, and not our mistake?"

He replied, "Yes."

So I said, "In that case you can just let us enter, correct?"

He gruffly replied no, and left it at that. I returned to our car, and started venting my anger. Then I returned to the guard and started all over another two times. I came back to the car very upset. I told Patricia, "I know the Lord wants us in Czechoslovakia, and now it's getting too late to get there on time, even if they were to allow us through right now." Patricia gently reminded me that I had been teaching about offering the *"sacrifice of praise"* (see Hebrews 13:6), and suggested this might be the time to put into practice what I'd been teaching.

I retorted, "I don't want to offer a sacrifice of praise right now. I'm angry!"

But I knew in my heart that she was right. So I started offering a sacrifice of praise, and I kept on until I had peace in my heart again. Then I went back to the border guard, sure he would give a positive response now that my heart was in a better place. But once again, he refused my request. So I asked more specifically, "Is there anything we can do about this situation?"

He said, "Yes. You can go back to the nearest large city, go to the American consulate, and they can re-issue the visa copy that was torn out by mistake."

I excitedly asked, "When does it close?"

He replied coldly, "In a few minutes."

If he had only said that three hours before, when we first approached him, we would have had time to go to the consulate, return, cross the border, and make it to our meeting in Czechoslovakia on time!

Facing another night in Poland, we had to ask the Lord to help us miraculously find the home of the Polish leader and translator with whom we had stayed (he had not given us his address, for security's sake). Amazingly, we found his home. His wife came to the door. When I explained our situation and asked if we could spend the night, she replied, "I knew you were coming back!" When I asked how she knew, she explained that right after we'd left, she had said to her husband that they really should have opened up with us and explained that their marriage was in great jeopardy, and that they were seriously considering divorcing. She had prayed we would come back!

Patricia prayed and ministered to her, and I to her husband. They both came to a place of personal repentance and forgave each other. We left them to share and pray with each other while we went to bed. The next morning, they said they really felt their marriage had been healed. Today, thirty-four years later, they are still together.

The next day we went to the American consulate, got the missing visa page replaced, and easily crossed the border into Czechoslovakia. When we arrived at the farm where they were to have had the meeting the night before, I profusely apologized for not being there, and explained what had happened.

The leader replied, "There was no problem at all. The Holy Spirit told us you would not arrive yesterday evening, and to tell all the believers to come the next evening instead. So you are here right on time, and they are waiting inside for you to minister to them."

Many times through the years, we have needed to remember that incident—to not get angry with God for not doing things the way we thought He should, or in the time frame that we expected of Him. We had to learn to offer a sacrifice of praise until our hearts could come into a place of trust and peace. We, like David, needed to continually inquire of the Lord. And every time, we eventually have seen that He is in control, and that His ways and His timing are higher than ours.

Inquiring of the Lord should always be a central part of our relationship with Him. Instead of forging ahead with what we think He wants and what we think is best, we need to ask Him what He thinks about any given situation, and especially about His house of prayer. When we allow Him to build His house through us, His house will stand. He will provide for His house. He will maintain His house. And as we learn to walk humbly with the Lord in this place of dependence and relationship, He will enable us to prepare a dwelling place for His Presence that will bring great change to our city and nation.

CONCLUSION

The Power of His Presence
Changes Cities and Nations

As we bring this book to a close, we want to emphasize that the main thing is not houses of prayer, or shifting cities or nations. It's not even worship or prayer. The main thing is the Lord Himself. It is only His Presence that can change a city or nation in lasting ways. We are merely seeking, like David, to prepare a dwelling place for Him in our city and nation—and in our hearts.

King David had to lay down selfish ambition and building his own kingdom in order to build the Kingdom of God. He had to yield to the Lord's discipline in order to come to that place of weakness where the Lord could show Himself strong and receive all the glory.

It is worth noting that when the ark was brought back successfully, it was brought back corporately. No one person could get all the glory for carrying the ark. They had to bring it back as a group who had learned to walk under authority, and who carried it in unity, keeping step together. No one could run ahead, and no one could lag behind. They had to die to self, and learn how to move forward together as a unit.

This time, rather than starting out with great fanfare celebrating his wealth and strength, King David sacrificed seven bulls and seven

> **To bring in God's manifested Presence, we must die to self, and to our flesh.**

rams (see 1 Chronicles 15:26). Some say the Hebrew could mean that he offered a sacrifice every seven steps. In any case, this successful bringing up of the ark was done in a spirit of humility, with a visible demonstration of symbols of fleshly strength (bulls and rams) being put to death. *To bring in God's manifested Presence, we must die to self, and to our flesh.*

Death to Self Releases the Joy of the Lord

But this procession was not some sad, funeral-like dirge. This true death to self released the genuine joy of the Lord:

12b So David went to bring up the ark of God from the house of Obed-Edom to the City of David with rejoicing. ... 14 Wearing a linen ephod, David was dancing before the Lord with all his might, 15 while he and all Israel were bringing up the ark of the Lord with shouts and the sound of trumpets. (2 Samuel 6:12b; 14–15)

This was the genuine joy of the Lord that comes after a time of correction and a right response to that discipline. The joy of the Lord is much deeper and more powerful than the joy we may feel when all is going our way. It is the deep, strong joy that comes when things are going His way!

The joy of the Lord that King David entered into is offensive to those who hold on to their dignity and their desire to impress others with their position, wealth, or strength. Such was the case with David's wife Michal:

16 As the ark of the Lord was entering the City of David, Michal daughter of Saul watched from a window. And when she saw King David leaping and dancing before the Lord, she despised him in her heart. .... 20 When David returned home to bless his household, Michal daughter of Saul came out to meet him and said, "How the king of Israel has distinguished himself today, going around half-naked in full view of the slave girls of his servants as any vulgar fellow would!" 21 David said to Michal, "It was before the Lord, who chose me rather than your father or anyone from his house when he appointed me ruler over the Lord's people Israel—I will celebrate before the Lord. 22 I will become even more undignified than this, and I will be humiliated in my own eyes. But by these slave girls you spoke of, I will be held in honor." 23 And Michal daughter of Saul had no children to the day of her death. (2 Samuel 6:16; 20–23)

One of the clearest models of becoming *"even more undignified than this"* was a dear brother who had a big impact on my life, the late Arthur Wallis. Arthur to me was the epitome of the stereotypical British gentleman. He spoke and moved with nobility and class. He was a polished orator in the best of the British tradition, and the author of many anointed books that spoke into my life.

I was amazed in 1985 to find myself on stage with him at the South and West Bible Week in England. We had been invited to that Bible Week event to present a musical we had written called "Celebrate His Holiness," and I had been invited to speak. But I believe most of us were there anticipating the deep and meaty teaching of Arthur Wallis.

During one of the worship times, Arthur was sitting in his typical, dignified fashion. But when a strong anointing came on a joyful song of praise, Arthur raised himself slowly, but then began to dance exuberantly to the Lord, flailing his long arms and legs in the air as he joyfully celebrated His Lord!

I was inspired by Arthur's freedom to lay aside a dignity that so many others aspired to, and to be *"more undignified than this"*. I believe it was in part because of his freedom from seeking to promote himself and his deep revelation of the grace of God.

His Presence Is by Grace

To bring in the ark of His Presence, we need the revelation of His grace. If we think we can build a house of prayer, be part of restoring the Tabernacle of David in our time, and help change cities or nations in our own strength, we are sadly mistaken. *Only by His grace* will these glorious things come to pass.

King David had the strongest revelation of grace that is given to us in the Old Testament. This is seen clearly, for example, in Psalm 103:10–14:

> *10 He does not treat us as our sins deserve or repay us according to our iniquities. 11 For as high as the heavens are above the earth, so great is His love for those who fear Him; 12 as far as the east is from the west, so far has He removed our transgressions from us. 13 As a father has compassion on his children, so the Lord has compassion on those who fear Him; 14 for He knows how we are formed, He remembers that we are dust.*

> **To bring in the ark of His Presence, we need the revelation of His grace.**

King David came to a place of great security because of his revelation of the grace of the Lord. This is evident in his response to Michal. He did not deny his royalty, but he realized deeply that his royalty was only a gift given by grace. He did not cling to his position or pursue selfish ambition. Rather, he acknowledged that he was in a position to glorify the One Who had placed Him there, the One Who alone is worthy of all praise and honor.

The Key to Shifting a City or Nation

Ministry to the Lord is the heart and foundation of any house of prayer that will have an impact on a city or nation—and the nations.

A worship leader named Gary Benjamin came to Succat Hallel for a year to learn and prepare to birth a house of prayer in a key European city. He had been the main worship leader in a church in America of about two thousand people. Then he was asked to serve as senior pastor. When he obeyed the call of God to go overseas to minister, he sold a beautiful home with a jacuzzi, cars, etc., and gave up a good salary to live by faith.

One morning, he was getting ready to lead a worship watch. Since we are 24/7, we have very few watches with large groups of people.

As he came into the room, he realized there were only three older ladies there. When he sat down at the piano. his mind was flooded with thoughts that he was crazy to have given up so much for so little. He was questioning whether he had really heard the Lord.

Just as he was about to start leading worship, he heard the sound of a large number of angels filling the room. It was as if he could hear angel wings rustling. He then thought he heard an angel near him say: "Shhh, he's about to start." He was shocked by this, as he normally did not see visions or into the spirit realm. He wondered if it was real.

Then one of the ladies came up to him and said: "I am so sorry to interrupt you, but I just have to tell you that when you sat down at the piano, I saw angels filling up the room. I heard the rustling of their wings. Then I heard one angel near you say, 'Shhh, he's about to start.'"

The worship leader said that experience quickly blew away any thoughts of regret. Even though he had taught on the priority of "ministry to the Lord" in the past, it took on a new level of revelation and experience for him.

If we are called to build the house of prayer through all the times when worship or prayer flow freely, and the times when they are a sacrifice; through times of miraculous financial provision, and times of need, and to persevere through all the joyful and difficult times; then we have to operate from a heart revelation that *His Presence is worth it all.*

A Blessing for You From Zion, His Holy Hill

May the Lord God of Zion reveal His grace and favor deep within your heart. May He graciously bring you to the place of total dependency upon Him, and upon Him alone. May you be part of fulfilling His purposes in your generation.

May you know where He has positioned you for each season of your life. May You become a house of prayer and part of building His house of prayer where He has placed you. May you be a part of bringing the ark of His Presence to a central place in your city and your nation.

May you be part of building a house of prayer that will help shift cities and nations. And may you be part of building the Throne for the Son of David, and extending His rule and reign over the earth.

In the all-powerful Name of Yeshua Ha Mashiah (Jesus, the Anointed One). Amen.

English Glossary

Ben Hinnom Valley
Literally, Son of Hinnom, the original Jebusite landowner. Over time, *Ge-Hinnom* (Hebrew for Valley of Hinnom) became known as "hell," a place of everlasting destruction, due to the sacrifice of children to the pagan god Molech, and continually burning fires to consume the city's refuse, including the dead bodies of animals and criminals and other filth.

Bridal
An intimate worship and devotional approach derived from the biblical relationship that believers as the "bride" have with the Lord as "bridegroom" (see Rev. 19:7-9; 21:9; 22:19).

City of David
The ancient urban core of Jerusalem in the fourth century B.C,. a narrow ridge descending south from the Temple Mount. Here **King David** captured the Jebusite fortress, established his capital, and pitched a tent for the ark.[10]

Crown and throne
Worship and prayer from the standpoint of believers' call to function as "kings" (1 Pet. 2:9; Rev. 5:10) who sit in the gates of cities and nations to execute and administer the decrees of the King of Kings (see chapter 14).

Governmental worship and intercession
Expresses the kingship of Jesus, His Throne, and the establishment of His kingdom or government over a city or nations.

Hamas
A Palestinian, Islamist terrorist organization in the Gaza Strip, which borders the Mediterranean Sea, Israel and Egypt.

---

10   https://www.seetheholyland.net/city-of-david/

Harp and bowl

An expression of the priestly role of the believer by combined prayer and worship to the Lord, as in Rev. 5:8. (See also "crown and throne"; and chapter 14.)

Isaiah 19 highway

Isaiah 19:23-25 speaks of Israel, Egypt, and ancient Assyria, today much of the Middle East. It is a foundation for prayer that God's prophetic purposes be released and established via "highways" bringing intercessors and worshippers, and establishing houses of prayer in this strategic area. (See chapters 16 and 17.)

Jesus People movement

"A wave of Christianity that began on the U.S. West Coast in the late 1960s and early 1970s and spread through North America and Europe, before subsiding in the early 1980s. It was the major evangelical Christian element in the hippie counterculture, or, conversely, the major hippie element within some strands of Protestantism. Members of the grass roots movement were called *Jesus People*."[11]

The Land

A name for Israel.

Mantle

An anointed calling, office and authority granted by the Lord to specific believers to fulfill His purposes.

Messiah

Hebrew for "anointed one," especially one consecrated for a special role. "Christ" is from the Greek word for "anointed."

Messianic

One meaning is Jews who believe Jesus Christ is the messiah for both Jew and Gentile, the One Who fulfills the promises of the Scriptures, from Genesis to Revelation.

---

11 Goll, James. "*What We Can Learn from the Jesus People*," *Charisma*; April 20, 2015. https://www.charismamag.com/blogs/a-voice-calling-out/23102-what-we-can-learn-from-the-jesus-people

Mountain of society

A specific area or pillar of culture that needs the salt and light of the kingdom of God, often defined as business, government, media, arts and entertainment, education, family and religion.

Mount Zion

The original Mount Zion was the eastern part of the Jebusite fortress that **King David** captured and called the City of David (see 2 Sam. 5:6-9). The location of the name "Mount Zion" changed twice. The Temple Mount was called Mount Zion when Solomon built the Temple. In the first century A.D., after the Romans destroyed Jerusalem, the name was moved to its present location, a hill across the Tyropoeon Valley.[12]

Old City

Jerusalem's crowded and vibrant Old City of about one square kilometer is enclosed by walls built in the sixteenth century by Suleiman the Magnificent. It is divided into Jewish, Christian, Armenian and Muslim quarters.

Shabbat

The Jews' Sabbath day of rest beginning at sundown Friday and ending at sundown Saturday.

Shofar

A ram's-horn trumpet used in Jewish religious ceremonies, once used as a battle signal, and now blown at Rosh Hashanah (the Jewish New Year) and Yom Kippur (the Day of Atonement). The shofar is used in some messianic and Christian congregations.

Sultan's Pool

A large water reservoir named after the Ottoman Sultans who built it, which once contributed to the water supply of Jerusalem.

Temple Mount

Believed to be Mount Moriah, where God tested Abraham, asking Him to offer Isaac, and the site of Solomon's Temple. Prophetically, it is the place of the Throne of the Lord, where He will place all

---

12   https://www.seetheholyland.net/mount-zion/

His enemies under His feet, and from where He will rule and reign forever on His holy hill.

Western Wall

Part of the Old City's retaining wall that Herod I built in 20 B.C., it is considered the sole remnant of the Temple. For fear of standing on the Holy of Holies, observant Jews do not ascend the Temple Mount, but worship at its Western Wall.[13]

13　https://www.seetheholyland.net/western-wall/

Hebrew Glossary

Adar
The twelfth month of the Hebrew calendar, corresponding to March-April.

Aliyah
Immigration to Israel, from the word "ascent," or "mount up."

Adonai
God or Lord.

Ashdod
Formerly a Philistine city on the Mediterranean Sea in southern Israel. Today it is Israel's largest modern port.

Barukh ha Shem
Blessed be the Name (of the Lord).

Intifada, Second
An armed, violent uprising by Palestinians against Israel, initiated and spurred on by Palestinian leaders in the West Bank and Gaza (2000-2005). The First Intifada (1987 to 1992) is not mentioned in this book.

Mashiah
Messiah. From a word meaning "anointed with oil," and thus consecrated. The word "Christ" is from the Greek word "anointed."

Mishkant Tsiyon
"Habitation of Zion." A 24/7 Korean house of prayer in northern Jerusalem.

Mo'adim
God's appointed or set times and feast days. (See Lev. 23:2,4).

Molech
(From the Hebrew word *melech*, meaning "king.") The false idol god of the Ammonites, to whom children were offered as burnt sacrifices. The hollow brass figure had outstretched arms heated

by a red-hot fire within, and the little ones placed in its arms were slowly burned. To prevent parents from hearing the cries of their dying children, the sacrificing priests beat drums.[14]

Olim
Immigrants.

Omer
A dry measure, sheaf (of grain), or grain offering.

Rosh Hodesh
The first day of the month, according to the Hebrew calendar.

Shavu'ot
The biblical feast of Pentecost, fulfilled when the Holy Spirit was poured out. (See Acts 2:1-21.)

Succat Hallel
Tent of Praise. A 24/7 house of prayer in southern Jerusalem overlooking the Temple Mount.

Sukkot
The Feast of Tabernacles, a major Jewish holiday commemorating the Israelites dwelling in booths (tabernacles or tents) in the wilderness (see Lev. 23:34-35). Many Bible scholars believe the Lord will fulfill this feast when He returns to "tabernacle" with His people and rule over the nations.

Topheth
A place at the southern end of the Ben Hinnom Valley, which means "place of fire or cremation," or possibly, is derived from "drum," since the idolatrous priests beat loudly on drums to drown out the screams of the children as they were sacrificed to the false god Molech.

Yeshua ha Mashiah
Jesus Christ.

---

14   http://classic.net.bible.org/dictionary.php?word=MOLECH

About the Authors

Rick and Patricia Ridings are based in Jerusalem, where they founded and lead *Succat Hallel*, a ministry that lifts up worship and intercession, 24 hours a day from their facility overlooking the Temple Mt. and Mt. Zion. *Succat Hallel* is known for youth worship and training bringing together hundreds of Jewish, Arab, and Palestinian youth. They have ministered extensively encouraging houses of prayer across the Middle East.

Rick and Patricia are considered leaders in the global prayer and worship movement. Their passion is to see a generation raised up that will give themselves fully in love and ministry to the Lord and who will serve the purposes of God in their generation.

Rick and Patricia have ministered on GOD TV, TBN, CBN, and in over 40 nations, speaking for churches, conferences, Bible and leadership training schools. They have three daughters, all in worship ministry, two of them on earth, and one in heaven. They have fourteen grandchildren.

www.succathallel.com